THE GOURMET
POTLUCK

THE GOURMET
POTLUCK

Show-Stopping Recipes for the Buffet Table

Beth Hensperger

PHOTOGRAPHY BY

Scott Peterson

TEN SPEED PRESS
Berkeley | Toronto

Ten Speed Press
Box 7123
Berkeley, California 94707
www.tenspeed.com

Distributed in Australia by Simon and Schuster Australia, in Canada by Ten Speed Press Canada,
in New Zealand by Southern Publishers Group, in South Africa by Real Books,
and in the United Kingdom and Europe by Airlift Book Company.

Cover and text design: Catherine Jacobes Design
Photography assistance: Tiffany Fosnight
Food styling: Jen Straus
Food styling assistance: Alexa Hyman
Prop styling: Peggi Jeung

Permission to include Scalloped Potatoes with Sage (page 71), adapted from Julee Rosso's
Scalloped Potatoes in *Great Good Food,* courtesy of Three Rivers Press.

Library of Congress Cataloging-in-Publication Data
Hensperger, Beth.
The gourmet potluck : show-stopping recipes for the buffet table / Beth Hensperger ;
photography by Scott Peterson.
p. cm.
Summary: "A collection of straightforward, sophisticated recipes scaled to serve 8
to 36 people, each including prep timeline, serving dishes and utensils needed, transportation
notes, and reheating requirements"—Provided by publisher.
Includes index.
ISBN-13: 978-1-58008-741-4 (pbk.)
ISBN-10: 1-58008-741-8 (pbk.)
1. Quantity cookery. 2. Buffets (Cookery) I. Title.
TX820.H46 2006
641.5'7—dc22   2005029670
Printed in China
First printing, 2006

1 2 3 4 5 6 7 8 9 10 — 10 09 08 07 06

To my mother, Phyllis Hensperger,
and her sister, Joan "Aunt Joan" Billheimer—
two girls who really know how to set a table
and feed a crowd with delicious style.

CONTENTS

INTRODUCTION

The word *potluck* has been in the English language since 1592. Originally, it described a meal offered to a guest that was literally the luck of the pot: the guest would choose from the items offered on the table—that is, whatever happened to be in the pot—rather than order specific dishes. I imagine an extra-long table set out under the trees, or in front of a cozy fireplace, with all manner of covered casseroles, overflowing platters, and full baskets celebrating an abundant harvest and good company.

Potluck has evolved into a cooperative group meal that is now a style of entertaining. It is by tradition made up of a variety of mixed and matched dishes brought by the guests. This style of eating not only is economical, but it also gives guests the opportunity to taste some wonderful dishes they might not ever make themselves. A large number of guests can be served without requiring one person to do all the work, while adding an element of surprise, all in one sweep. A host or hostess can leave all the elements to fate or allocate a specific dish to each person, preferably matching up guests with their specialties, which can elevate a simple meal into the remarkable.

I've designed this cookbook to inspire cooks of all levels with new ideas for stylish, nutritious dishes for group entertaining. Some cooks might already have a well-tested repertoire of recipes designed to feed a crowd, but most cooks I know always enjoy asking each other for ideas and mulling over new possibilities. Others might experience some anxiety at the thought of preparing food for a group, often expending more energy worrying about impressing others rather than simply nourishing them. The good news is that a tasty, well-executed, simple dish will always outshine an overly ambitious one. The easy-to-make recipes I've selected should help allay those fears.

Many features set this cookbook apart. The recipes include dishes to feed a wide range of groups, whether for an intimate gathering or for a large buffet. So, when you receive your next potluck-dinner invitation, you can reach for this book and have plenty of choices at your fingertips rather than scramble through many books for something appropriate, adjusting recipes accordingly. You'll find well-proven delicious and easy-to-prepare homemade dishes that have a wide appeal and can transport well.

A number of helpful notes accompany each recipe, designed to highlight the preparation, transporting, and serving details. These notes include information and advice about what serving dishes and utensils to bring, what you can make ahead, how to plan your preparation time, how to transport with no mess, and what last-minute assembly or reheating might be required. This way you can easily skim the recipes to find just the right dish for the event, whether you are invited to a barbecue at the beach, a casual evening at a friend's home, or a charity dinner at the community hall.

Because menu planning involves more than the size of the group or the level of formality, I have organized the recipes by season so you can quickly find recipes that have just the right appeal and mood for each occasion. Seasonal cooking is not intimidating, but practical and interesting. For example, when you are invited to a New Year's Eve party, you'll have a rich array of substantial and savory winter menu ideas on hand to choose from, such as Moroccan Chicken with Dried Fruit and Olives (page 79) or Salmon en Croûte (page 75). Or when you get that summer picnic invitation, just flip to the summer section for fresh and light selections, like Cold Baked Chicken Breasts with Jalapeño Plum Sauce (page 36) or Calico Bean Bake (page 47). In choosing main and side dishes for each season, I opted for sensible, delicious recipes, often regional in origin, that are appetizing to a wide range of palates.

I notice my creativity really comes alive when cooking with the purpose of sharing with friends. The idea of gourmet food should never overwhelm but delight the senses and inspire. The possibilities are endless and the choices are yours.

Gourmet Potluck How-To Guide: What Can I Bring?

At some point each of us has been called upon to either organize a buffet for a crowd or bring a prepared dish to a gathering of friends. Holiday celebrations, New Year's Eve buffets, office parties, baby showers, professional committee meetings, sports events (from tail-gates to Little League victory parties), Friday night card games, school or church gatherings, barbecues, and countless other get-togethers usually have one thing in common: good food.

When asked to bring food to a gathering, you might quickly brush over the details of the invitation and fall back on the same old recipe or plan on one quick stop at the supermarket deli. But in reality, selecting the right dish for a potluck requires a multi-step process of elimination and decisions. This isn't a difficult or time-consuming thing to do, but the success of your edible contribution depends on making the right choices. No one wants to see their culinary creation languishing on the buffet table at the end of the party, untouched by the other guests.

For your convenience, I have broken down this simple process sequentially. This checklist will enable you to select the appropriate style of food for any occasion. This may sound like a lot to remember, but if you think logically about the step-by-step procedures of potluck, it will soon become second nature to you. Once this is done, it's on to the fun part: selecting the perfect recipe!

TYPE OF EVENT AND TIME OF DAY

To identify the type of event your host envisions, do a little detective work. (If you are the host, be sure to offer this information to your guests bringing food.) Food served at a fancy black-tie buffet should differ significantly from that chosen for an outdoor tailgate party in the parking lot of the local sports arena.

* Is it a brunch, lunch, dinner, office party, birthday party, bridal shower, or an evening dinner buffet?

* Will this be held in a private home (indoors or outside?) or in an office, public recreation center, a skating rink, or church hall?

* Will guests be able to sit down for the meal or will they have to hold a plate while standing?

* Are you familiar with the other guests, and what is your common bond? (A room full of long-haul truck drivers may not appreciate a cannelloni when they could have chili. You don't want to bring a cold roast of veal to a group of predominantly vegetarians.)

* Will the group be exclusively adults or will there also be children? (Grandmas usually have different party-food expectations than six-year-olds do.)

NUMBER OF GUESTS

The host should let you know if your contribution will be part of a casual taste-of-this-and-that or if your dish needs to be the proper size to adequately feed all of the guests. What you choose to serve ten will differ markedly from what you might offer a crowd of fifty.

TIME OF YEAR AND AVAILABILITY

For both economy and maximum flavor, try to cook according to the seasons. Consider the season of the year and the foods that are readily available at that time. The tomatoes that your friends raved about in August would be an anemic, flavorless choice for a February potluck. Hard winter squash, brussels sprouts, and chestnuts are rarely available—or appropriate—for a summer gathering, nor is fresh corn or asparagus available at Thanksgiving.

THE TYPE OF MENU

It's okay to be a little nosy. Ask the host what else is being served and complement what is already on the menu. There's no point in bringing your famous Mexican green chile tortilla casserole if three other people are bringing their special Mexican casseroles too. If you have a particular specialty, be polite and ask whether the host considers it appropriate for the occasion. Also be sure to ask about guests' special dietary needs and food allergies. Ingredients like pork, shellfish, coconut, garlic, or peanuts can be disastrous if someone is allergic.

THE ON-SITE FACILITY AND LAST-MINUTE PREPARATION

Ask in advance whether refrigerator space, a stove top, microwave, oven, or even counter space will be available to you. This is imperative if your dish requires any special handling to store, heat, slice, or otherwise finish before serving.

Easiest Dishes: Pasta, cold sliced filet of beef, stuffed chicken breasts, chicken drumsticks, layered casseroles with cooked rice, enchiladas, canned-bean chili.

Most Difficult Dishes: Anything with puff pastry on the outside and meat on the inside, pasta or vegetable casseroles with multiple sauce preparations, or fussy sauces that can lump or curdle when reheated or that must be served at a specific temperature.

Least Expensive Dishes: Chicken, beans, canned tuna, pasta, tortillas, polenta, sauces with canned tomatoes, seasonal vegetables, and crêpes.

Most Expensive Dishes: Veal, beef, lamb, sushi, prawns, salmon, wild rice, dried mushrooms, and any specialty vegetable out of season.

Equipment—Be Prepared

Of course, you need the proper equipment to prepare your dish at home, but also consider whether you have an appropriate bowl, platter, or casserole in which to transport and serve your dish. The formality of the occasion will dictate how fancy, homey, or rustic your contribution should appear.

Over the decades, I have found that searching out basic, practical serving platters and bowls in advance is worth the time and expense. There is rarely time to purchase suitable tableware the day of the function. A last-minute search for the proper serving platter can prove futile even in the most well-stocked temple of gastronomy. Best to stock up in advance on items that appeal to you; it won't be long before you'll be using them.

Breakability is a big factor. For casual occasions, baskets can't be beat, since they are lightweight and look great on the buffet. You can use baskets not only as a platter for cheese or crudités but also to hold casserole dishes. Sturdy baskets with handles are also elegant substitutes for cardboard boxes, plastic tubs, or paper bags.

There is also a world of plastic out there, everything from chic designer-inspired creations to the sort of thing you might use to feed the family pet. Large warehouse stores and restaurant supply houses carry a staggering array of heavy-duty plastic equipment, from inexpensive supersize faux-crystal salad bowls to all sorts of rimmed platters in a variety of colors. Stock up on sturdy plastic containers with snap-on lids. If they break or get lost, you won't fret because they are easily and inexpensively replaced.

To ensure the return of your personal nondisposable treasures and containers, label the bottom with your full name printed on heavy-duty tape.

Always pack the appropriate serving utensils, since few hosts own enough large serving spoons or cute little spreading knives to accommodate all the dishes that comprise a buffet. When taking equipment out of your home, there is always the chance it will get lost, so don't pack your great-grandmother's vintage sterling pie server unless you're willing to risk losing it. Again, restaurant supply houses are a great resource for oversize spoons and spatulas, from the utilitarian to the downright attractive.

CASSEROLE SIZE	OVENPROOF BAKING DISH EQUIVALENT
1 quart	6 by 8 by 1½-inch baking dish or 6-inch soufflé dish
1½ quart	8 by 8 by 2-inch baking dish or 7-inch soufflé dish
2 quart	9 by 9 by 2-inch baking dish or 8-inch soufflé dish
2½ quart	10 by 10 by 2-inch baking dish or 9-inch soufflé dish
3 to 4 quart	9 by 13-inch or 10 by 10 by 4-inch baking dish or 10-inch soufflé dish
5 quart	15 by 10 by 2-inch baking dish or 12- to 14-inch round or oval gratin dish
6 quart	16 by 14 by 3-inch baking dish or 17- to 18-inch round or oval gratin dish

Try to find easy-to-use serving utensils that allow buffet guests to serve themselves efficiently. (For example, when you are holding a buffet plate in your hand, scissors-type salad servers make picking up lettuce leaves far easier than separate forks and spoons ever could.) Similarly, always precut your buffet foods, like stuffed chicken breasts, into serving-size portions.

Above is a guide to the approximate casserole dish equivalents. I think you will find it useful.

Transportation—Getting It There and Home Again

You have chosen an appropriate dish, you've made your lists, and the day approaches, but there is one more consideration: how to transport your completed dish to the celebration.

Over the years, I have had my share of oversize salad bowls propped precariously on the front car seat, casseroles laid on or wrapped in a large towel on the car floor or inside a cardboard box in the trunk. The idea is to get a dish from point A to B without spilling or dumping the contents. One major spill can leave your auto upholstery with a not-so-pleasant memory and you without your contribution to the buffet.

My motto is don't take anything for granted. Transporting food is a tricky business. You need to plan accordingly, pack well, and drive carefully. When figuring out what to bring, consider whether your perfect presentation dish will also stay steady in the car.

In many instances, you may want to contribute a fully prepared dish that is served at room temperature. In that case, you will be transporting only one platter or casserole dish, often the vessel in which the food was cooked. Casseroles are one of the most easily carried containers. When it's a large party, consider making two duplicate items rather than one large one. Not only will two smaller serving dishes be easier to maneuver; when one dish is empty on the buffet, you can replace it with the remaining full one. This way only half as many guests will be faced with the sorry sight of a half-empty casserole or tepid food when they travel through the buffet line.

The best way to carry a steaming hot casserole of any size is to first cover with foil and then wrap it in a large towel. It is also incredibly easy to carry up and down stairs, and your dish will stay nice and hot.

The basic tenet of food safety is to keep hot foods hot and cold foods cold. Always plan for this. Consider investing in one of the many types of insulated thermal totes on the market or in one of the various sizes of ice chests. You may be surprised to know that ice chests are perfect for keeping hot food hot as well as cold food chilled: if that dish is already piping hot, it will stay so for hours if packed correctly in a cooler. Rival Company, maker of slow cookers, sells an insulated tote bag specifically made for transporting its crockery inserts. This tote is great for not only bringing the stuffing or stew you made in the slow cooker but also carrying soups transferred to plastic containers with tight lids. You can also effectively transport hot foods in cardboard boxes or baskets lined with newspapers or towels.

If a dish needs some last-minute assembling or heating, you will not only be bringing the serving dish, but possibly all the ingredients not yet added, garnishes, even equipment needed to do last-minute cooking. I usually pack all this in a large canvas tote or sturdy handled paper shopping bag for transporting, and I always make a packing list.

At the end of the dinner, you may have leftover food to bring home. It is good form to offer leftovers to the host, but often, the host will beg you to take your leftover food home. If you can wash your dish and utensil at the party site, all the better, but often this is simply not an option. Be prepared to carry the bowl home, full and funky, to clean up in your own kitchen.

To simplify your life, pack a medium plastic drawstring garbage bag (it will easily fit in your purse, pocket, or carrying tote) and slide the dish into the bag, tying it closed to prevent any spills on the way home. If there is a breakable platter or casserole at stake, surround the bag with the same padding material you used to get it there. If you brought a serving utensil, also pack a separate plastic bag to carry it home.

BOUNTIFUL SPRING BUFFET

WINE-BRAISED BRISKET

SERVES 12 *Braised brisket is so good and so popular, I am often left wondering why I don't see it on every potluck table. You can serve it as the meat course or pile it on fresh French rolls for sandwiches. While I don't usually use commercial mixes in my cooking, this brisket is so wildly popular I would be remiss to not let you in on this delightfully simple secret recipe that is so perfect for entertaining.*

❖ ❖ ❖

Preheat the oven to 325°F. Place the brisket in a large roasting pan or Dutch oven. Sprinkle with the soup mix and tomatoes and then top with the tomato sauce. Pour the wine over everything. Cover tightly with heavy-duty aluminum foil. (This is important to retain the juices.) If using a Dutch oven, place the cover over the foil for the tightest seal.

Bake in the center of the oven for 2 hours and then carefully open the foil and add the mushrooms. Recover and bake another 2 hours (4 hours total), until fork-tender. Remove the meat and mushrooms from the gravy and place in a shallow storage container. Cover and refrigerate overnight. Pour off the gravy and refrigerate in a storage container separately, also overnight.

The next day, before transporting, skim and discard the congealed fat from the cold gravy. Place the gravy in a small saucepan and boil to thicken; season with salt and pepper and cool.

Slice the meat across the grain into ³/₈-inch-thick slices. Arrange it in the large serving pan and top with the mushrooms. Pour the gravy over the top. Cover and refrigerate until ready to transport. Reheat on site.

TRANSPORTATION NOTES: Place the tightly covered roasting pan on the floor of the car or in the trunk with a large thick towel wrapped around the base to prevent tipping, or place in an insulated cooler for longer transport.

ON SITE/PREPARATION: Reheat at 350°F, covered with foil, for about 30 minutes, until warmed through. Serve immediately.

Preparation Timeline: **Best if made 1 day ahead and refrigerated overnight**

Serving Equipment: **10 by 10 by 4-inch ceramic roasting pan, serving fork, bowl and spoon or small ladle for the gravy**

On site/Reheat: **Yes**

On site/Refrigeration: **Optional**

Serving Temperature: **Warm**

---

1 (5-pound) beef brisket, trimmed of external fat

1 packet dehydrated onion soup mix

¹/₄ cup sundried tomatoes packed in oil, drained and chopped

1 (8-ounce) can tomato sauce

2 cups dry red wine

1¹/₂ pounds mushrooms, halved or quartered

Salt and freshly ground black pepper

OVEN-POACHED WHOLE SALMON

SERVES 16 *For salmon lovers, here is a spectacular special-occasion presentation with a bit of a ritual attached to it. It will be a welcome main course on a hot evening. Order a whole salmon from your fishmonger or good supermarket meat counter. It's a good idea to measure the length of the fish so you can be sure it will fit in your oven and on your platter or cutting board.*

＊ ＊ ＊

Preheat the oven to 400°F. Place 2 large baking sheets, upside down and next to each other, on the oven rack to support the fish while it bakes.

Slowly heat the wine in a saucepan over medium heat to boiling. Tear off 2 large pieces of heavy-duty aluminum foil the length of the fish plus 6 inches extra on both ends. Brush or spray the shiny side of one with oil and place on a cutting board. Center the fish on the foil. Using a ruler, measure the fish at the thickest part right behind the head (this will determine cooking time).

Turn the fish on its back and spread the cavity open. Season well with salt and pepper, tuck in the dill, and then arrange the lemon and onion wedges inside. Lay the fish back down on its side. Rub the entire surface of the fish with olive oil.

Bend the edges of the foil up and lay the other piece of foil over the top. Fold the edges together toward the fish and then tightly roll them to seal. Before sealing the last end section, carefully add the hot wine and then tightly roll to seal. (The foil should encase the fish loosely; leave the edges up and curled toward the fish to prevent drips.) Use the cutting board to help transfer the fish to the oven, carefully sliding the fish off the board and onto the baking sheets, taking care not to tear the foil or open the edges.

Preparation Timeline: The fish can be poached and refrigerated up to 2 days ahead

Serving Equipment: Large oval serving platter or cutting board, carving knife, oversize serving spatula

On site/Reheat: No

On site/Refrigeration: Optional

Serving Temperature: Chilled or room temperature

1 cup white wine or dry vermouth

1 (4$^1/_2$- to 5-pound) whole salmon with skin, head, and tail on; cleaned, rinsed, and patted dry

Salt and freshly ground black or white pepper

$^1/_2$ bunch fresh dill or thyme

1 to 2 lemons, cut into wedges

1 large white onion, cut into wedges

Olive oil

GARNISHES

3 lemons, sliced

1 or 2 cucumbers, peeled and sliced

2 bunches curly parsley

2 bunches watercress

Bake the fish for 10 minutes for every inch of thickness, before testing for doneness. To test, carefully open the foil near the head and insert an instant-read thermometer behind the head at the thickest part; it should register 130°F to 140°F. A knife inserted into that portion should show no raw-red tinge near the backbone, and the flesh should flake easily. Turn off the oven, open the oven door, and slowly pull out the rack. Let the fish rest on the oven rack for 10 minutes before carefully transferring to a large cooling rack. Cool a bit and then refrigerate in the foil for up to 2 days.

Before transporting, open the foil carefully and gently peel off the skin on both sides and pour off any liquid; the fish should be firm. Reseal in the foil.

TRANSPORTATION NOTES: Transport the salmon wrapped tightly in foil in a large cardboard box or on thick towels. If a hot day, transport in a cooler. Bring the lemons, cucumbers, and herbs in plastic bags.

ON SITE/PREPARATION: Arrange the parsley and watercress on the long serving platter. Remove the fish from the foil and place it on the platter. Decorate with lemon and cucumber slices around the edges. Serve immediately or refrigerate to serve chilled. To serve, use the carving knife to cut gently along the seam of the backbone running the full length of the fish. Cut crosswise into portions and use the knife and serving spatula to lift the pieces off the bone. Turn the fish over to serve the bottom half.

SHRIMP with FETA

SERVES 15 *Shrimp is one of those special party foods that make people light up when they see them. No cheese really goes with shrimp like sharp, salty feta, and this bountiful dish is a classic in traditional Greek cooking. Make this in two casseroles to keep the shrimp in a shallow layer.*

◆ ◆ ◆

To make the sauce, heat the oil in a deep heavy saucepan over medium heat. Add the onions and sauté until soft, about 5 minutes. Add the garlic and cook a few minutes until soft but not browned. Add the tomatoes, tomato paste, jalapeño, basil, oregano, sugar, and salt. Bring to a boil, then decrease the heat to achieve a high simmer. Cook, stirring occasionally, for about 30 minutes, until thickened. Remove from the heat and allow to cool to room temperature. Cover and refrigerate for up to 1 week.

Place the 2 casseroles near your work area. Working in batches, melt 4 tablespoons of the butter over high heat in a sauté pan. Add half the shrimp and sauté until it just turns pink, no more, about $1^1/_2$ minutes. Add 1 to 2 tablespoons of the ouzo and 2 to 4 tablespoons of the brandy, turn the heat to high (or carefully flame with a long-handled match), and quickly cook until the alcohol evaporates. Pour the shrimp and butter into 1 of the casseroles. Repeat with the rest of the butter, shrimp, ouzo, and brandy.

Pour the tomato sauce over the shrimp to cover (for a drier casserole, use only some of the sauce). Sprinkle each casserole with the feta. Cover with foil and refrigerate for up to 8 hours before transporting.

Preparation Timeline: The sauce can be made up to 1 week ahead and the casserole can be prepared up to 8 hours ahead, if refrigerated

Serving Equipment: Two 4-quart or 10 by 10 by 4-inch casseroles, large serving spoon

On site/Reheat: Yes

On site/Refrigeration: Yes, if not baking immediately

Serving Temperature: Hot or warm

GREEK TOMATO SAUCE

$^1/_3$ cup olive oil

3 large yellow onions, chopped

6 cloves garlic, minced

4 (28-ounce) cans crushed tomatoes, undrained

$^1/_3$ cup tomato paste

1 medium or 2 small jalapeño chiles, stemmed, seeded, and finely chopped

$^1/_4$ cup chopped fresh basil

$1^1/_2$ tablespoons chopped fresh oregano

2 teaspoons sugar

$1^1/_2$ teaspoons salt

TRANSPORTATION NOTES: Place the foil-wrapped casseroles on the floor of the car or in the trunk with a large thick towel wrapped around each base to prevent tipping, or place in an insulated cooler for longer transport. Refrigerate on site if not baking immediately. Carry the chopped parsley in a plastic sandwich bag.

ON SITE/PREPARATION: Preheat the oven to 400°F. Place the casseroles in the oven right before people hit the buffet; you don't want them to sit. Remove the foil and bake for 12 to 15 minutes, until the sauce is hot and bubbly and the cheese has melted; be careful not to overbake. Top with the chopped parsley. Serve immediately.

1 stick ($^1/_2$ cup) unsalted butter

4 pounds medium-large shrimp (about 90 shrimp), peeled, deveined, and tail on

$^1/_4$ cup ouzo

$^1/_2$ cup Greek brandy or Cognac

$1^1/_2$ pounds crumbled feta cheese ($4^1/_2$ cups)

$^1/_2$ cup chopped fresh flat-leaf parsley, for garnish

MUSTARDY GLAZED HAM

SERVES 16 TO 20 *Whether the occasion is glamorous or casual, a glazed ham is always a delight on the buffet table. The sweetness of this glaze is counterpoint to the savory saltiness. I prefer to make a half ham, using a bone-in shank portion or a boneless spiral-sliced ham, and cook it slowly, 12 to 14 minutes per pound, to keep it from drying out.*

◆ ◆ ◆

Preheat the oven to 300°F. Set the oven rack in the lowest position. Cut the netting off the ham, if necessary, and rinse the ham under cold water. Cut off and discard the tough outer skin and most of the fat, leaving a 1/4-inch-thick layer. Place the ham in a large, deep roasting pan and make long parallel cuts 1/4 inch deep and up to 1 inch apart all over the fatty side of the ham that will be facing up on the serving platter; then give it a quarter turn and repeat in the opposite direction, making crosshatch incisions over the surface. Lay the bay leaves on top. Place the ham in the oven and roast, uncovered, for 1 hour.

To make the glaze, combine the marmalade, brown sugar, mustard, and honey in a bowl with a fork or whisk.

Remove the ham from the oven and increase the heat to 350°F. For a festive presentation, stud the ham with the cloves, inserting one at each crosshatch. With a wide pastry brush, generously brush the entire ham with about half the glaze and return it to the oven.

Cook the ham for another 45 to 60 minutes, brushing with the glaze 1 to 2 more times (about every 20 minutes). Remove the ham from the oven when the internal temperature reaches 120°F at the thickest part of the ham without touching the bone. The outside of the ham should be browned and the meat should be heated through. Tent the ham with foil and let rest for at least 30 minutes. Serve within 2 hours of roasting or remove the ham from the roasting pan, wrap in foil, and then chill until serving.

continued

Preparation Timeline: Can be made 1 day ahead, if refrigerated

Serving Equipment: Large platter or decorative carving board, meat fork, long knife, serving spoons for the mustards

On site/Reheat: Optional

On site/Refrigeration: No

Serving Temperature: Warm or room temperature

1 (7- to 9-pound) bone-in smoked ham or fully cooked boneless ham

2 bay leaves

ORANGE-HONEY-MUSTARD GLAZE

3/4 cup orange marmalade

3/4 cup (packed) light or dark brown sugar

1/2 cup Dijon mustard

1/4 cup honey

1 tablespoon whole cloves (optional)

Jars of different mustards, for serving

TRANSPORTATION NOTES: Transport the ham tightly wrapped in foil in a large paper or canvas shopping bag with handles. Bring along 1 or 2 jars of mustard to serve on the side.

ON SITE/PREPARATION: Serve at room temperature or reheat at 300°F, wrapped in foil and placed directly on the oven rack, for about 30 minutes, until heated through. Let rest before slicing. To serve, unwrap the ham and transfer it to the serving platter. Carve into thin slices at the table and place the jars of mustard on the side.

BONELESS STUFFED CHICKEN BREASTS

SERVES 24 *Stuffed chicken breasts are one of the most popular buffet main dishes I have ever made. You can make this recipe for one hundred, and it is just as easy to prepare, bake, and arrange on a platter. I usually cut the breasts in half for the perfect buffet portion and so the diner can see the delicious filling.*

◆ ◆ ◆

Melt the butter with the oil in a skillet over medium heat. Add the shallots and sauté until limp, about 10 minutes. Combine the ricotta, spinach, eggs, parsley, Italian herbs, and nutmeg in a bowl and season with salt and pepper. Add the shallots and mix until evenly distributed.

Preheat the oven to 375°F. Spray a large roasting pan with olive oil cooking spray. Place a chicken breast half with the skin-side up on a work surface. With your fingers, loosen the skin on 1 side to make a pocket. Stuff about 1/3 cup of the stuffing under the skin. Fold the skin down to encompass the filling. Place the breast, skin-side up, in the roasting pan. Continue to stuff all the breast halves and place them side by side in rows, touching each other, in the pan.

Bake, uncovered, for 30 to 40 minutes, until the outsides are golden brown, the juices run clear, and there is no pink inside. Cool in the pan to room temperature. (If making in advance, the chicken can be covered with foil and refrigerated at this point for up to 1 day.) To serve, slice the cooled breasts in half and arrange them on a platter. If you have a standup crowd, slice each breast into 4 thick slices and arrange on the platter in overlapping slices.

TRANSPORTATION NOTES: Tightly cover and place in a position to prevent tipping.

ON SITE/PREPARATION: Unwrap the platter and serve.

Preparation Timeline: **Can be made up to 1 day ahead, if refrigerated**

Serving Equipment: **Large platter, knife, serving fork**

On site/Reheat: **No**

On site/Refrigeration: **Optional**

Serving Temperature: **Chilled or cool room temperature**

1 tablespoon butter

2 tablespoons olive oil

2 medium to large shallots, chopped, or 1/2 cup chopped green onions, white and green parts

2 pounds whole milk ricotta cheese

2 (10-ounce) packages frozen chopped spinach, thawed and squeezed dry

2 large eggs, beaten

1/2 cup chopped fresh flat-leaf parsley

1 teaspoon dried Italian herbs

Large pinch of ground nutmeg

Pinch of salt

Freshly ground black or white pepper

16 boneless chicken breast halves with skin on, rinsed and patted dry

FILO GREEN TART with FRESH DILL and FETA

SERVES 12 *This impressive-looking tart, a version of the Greek spanako-pita, is a fabulous meatless dish for entertaining. Frozen filo dough is available in most supermarkets, but you may find fresh filo in a market specializing in Middle Eastern foods. Defrost the filo in the refrigerator in its plastic wrapper before using.*

◆ ◆ ◆

Heat 2 tablespoons of the olive oil in a small sauté pan over medium heat. Add the green onions and sauté until limp, about 2 minutes; set aside to cool.

In a large bowl with a wooden spoon or an electric mixer fitted with the paddle attachment, combine the feta, cottage cheese, and cream cheese. Stir in the eggs and mix well. Add the spinach, green onions, parsley, and dill. Season with salt and pepper.

Preheat the oven to 350°F. Coat the bottom and sides of the baking pan with olive oil spray. Pour the separated butter into a bowl or large measuring cup, discarding the solids, and add the remaining 2/3 cup olive oil. Lay the unfolded filo sheets on a work surface and cover with a clean damp tea towel to prevent them from drying out.

Place 1 sheet of filo in the pan so that a quarter of the sheet hangs over the rim. Lightly brush the entire sheet with the butter mixture. Repeat with 7 more sheets of filo, arranging them in an overlapping circular pattern to cover the entire bottom and sides of the pan. If your filo has holes or gets torn, just patch with another sheet or with scraps and brush with the butter. If a few of your filo sheets stick together, just use the stack and brush with extra butter.

Evenly spread the spinach filling into the lined pan. Brush another sheet of filo with the butter mixture and place it on top of the filling, again leaving a quarter of the sheet hanging over the rim. Repeat with 7 more sheets to create the top crust. Brush the top with

continued

Preparation Timeline: Can be assembled and baked up to 2 days ahead, if refrigerated, or can stand at room temperature for 4 to 6 hours after baking, if served the same day

Serving Equipment: 14-inch deep-dish pizza pan, tart pan, or paella pan; serving platter (optional); serving spatula

On site/Reheat: Optional

On site/Refrigeration: No

Serving Temperature: Warm or room temperature

2 tablespoons plus 2/3 cup olive oil

1 bunch green onions, white and some of the green parts, finely chopped, or 2 thin leeks, thinly sliced

1 pound 6 ounces feta, rinsed, drained, and crumbled

1 pound large-curd cottage cheese

1 (8-ounce) package cream cheese, at room temperature

6 large eggs, lightly beaten

4 (10-ounce) packages frozen spinach, thawed and squeezed dry

1/2 cup chopped fresh flat-leaf parsley

1/4 cup chopped fresh dill

Pinch of salt and freshly ground black pepper

1 1/2 sticks (3/4 cup) butter, melted and cooled to allow the solids to separate

butter. With your fingers, tuck the overhanging dough in around the edges and underneath the mixture so it forms part of the crust.

With a paring knife, score the pastry almost to the filling to mark 12 wedges. Place the milk in a small bowl. Dip 2 fingers into the milk and gently trace around the rim of the tart and along the scored lines (this will keep the crust from thrusting up and curling during baking), pressing gently to adhere the layers. Sprinkle with the sesame seeds, if desired.

Immediately place the tart in the hot oven and bake for 45 to 50 minutes, until golden and crisp. Remove from the oven and let cool for at least 30 minutes. Serve warm or room temperature, or tightly cover and refrigerate for up to 2 days.

TRANSPORTATION NOTES: Tightly wrap the fully cooked tart with foil and place it on the floor of the car or in the trunk with a large thick towel wrapped around the base to prevent tipping.

ON SITE/PREPARATION: Serve at room temperature or reheat, uncovered, at 350°F for 15 to 30 minutes, until warmed through and the filo is recrisped. Cut the tart into 12 wedges and serve in the pan or place the wedges on a serving platter.

1 pound filo pastry sheets (you will use 16 sheets; wrap and refreeze the remainder)

2 tablespoons milk

1 tablespoon sesame seeds (optional)

MÉLANGE of BABY VEGETABLES

SERVES 12 *Here is my favorite spring vegetable offering. It is different from other vegetable recipes in this collection because it is sautéed instead of baked. Baby vegetables are staples at farmers' markets and produce stands—summer squash with the blossoms attached, thin baby carrots with flowing greens, baby turnips, very small green beans, thin asparagus. Just mix and match.*

• • •

Place the vegetables in bowls or plastic storage bags according to their density: hard vegetables (carrots, turnips), medium vegetables (squash, asparagus), leafy greens (chard, turnip greens, baby green beans). Refrigerate until transporting or cooking.

In a large skillet over high heat, melt 1 tablespoon of the butter with 1 tablespoon of the oil, until bubbly. Add the red and yellow peppers first and sauté until softened and browned, about 3 minutes, stirring constantly. Adding equal parts butter and oil as you go, next add the carrots and turnips and sauté for about 5 minutes, until softened. Then add the squash and asparagus, cooking for 1 to 2 minutes. Then add the chard, turnip greens, and baby green beans. Cook, stirring and tossing constantly, until nice and hot, 5 to 10 minutes. You want all the vegetables to be just tender and heated thoroughly. Sprinkle with salt, toss to distribute, and then transfer right away to the serving dish. Cool to room temperature. Arrange the lemon wedges around the outside of the serving dish.

TRANSPORTATION NOTES: Tightly cover the cooled cooked vegetables in the serving dish with plastic wrap or transport the uncooked vegetables in plastic bags. Bring a sauté pan and metal tongs and carry the butter and olive oil in covered containers, if cooking on site.

ON SITE/PREPARATION: Unwrap the vegetables and serve at room temperature or sauté the vegetables on site, transfer to a serving platter or bowl, and serve immediately, garnished with the lemon wedges.

Preparation Timeline: Make the day of serving; best if sautéed on site

Serving Equipment: Large oval platter or shallow bowl, oversize serving spoon

On site/Reheat: No

On site/Refrigeration: No

Serving Temperature: Warm or room temperature

1 pound baby carrots, halved lengthwise, or 1 (16-ounce) package frozen baby carrots, thawed

$1/2$ pound baby turnips with greens reserved, halved

1 pound mixed baby summer squash with blossoms attached (such as zucchini, pattypan, or yellow), or small zucchini, cut into $1/2$-inch strips

1 pound thin asparagus, tough ends snapped, diagonally cut into 4-inch sections

1 bunch green Swiss chard, stem and 4 inches of the green, chopped

$1/2$ pound baby green beans, stemmed

1 red bell pepper, sliced into $1/4$-inch-wide strips

1 yellow bell pepper, sliced into $1/4$-inch-wide strips

6 tablespoons unsalted butter

$1/3$ to $1/2$ cup olive oil

Salt

4 lemons, cut into wedges, for garnish

ZUCCHINI al FORNO

SERVES 8 *I've taken this baked vegetable gratin to potluck suppers for years. I look for a sweet white or yellow onion, like a Maui, Vidalia, or Walla Walla—the kind of onion that is so sweet you can eat it like an apple. I usually bake it on site, but you can bake right before leaving the house instead.*

◆ ◆ ◆

Preheat the oven to 350°F, if baking immediately. Rub the gratin dish with olive oil or butter. Fill with overlapping slices of zucchini and onion, sprinkling them with the marjoram. Season with salt and a few grinds of pepper, then drizzle with the olive oil or dot the top with butter. Sprinkle with the Parmesan. Cover the gratin with foil. (If making ahead, the gratin can be refrigerated at this point. Allow the chilled gratin to return to room temperature before baking.)

Bake for 30 to 40 minutes, covered, until tender when pierced with the tip of a knife. Do not overbake.

TRANSPORTATION NOTES: Tightly cover and place in a position to prevent tipping.

ON SITE/PREPARATION: Remove the foil from the cooked gratin and serve warm or at room temperature. Or bake on site according to the directions above.

Preparation Timeline: Bake the day of serving

Serving Equipment: Shallow 3-quart casserole or gratin dish or 9 by 13-inch baking dish, oversize serving spoon

On site/Reheat: Optional

On site/Refrigeration: No

Serving Temperature: Hot, warm, or room temperature

8 (8- to 11-inch-long) zucchini, diagonally cut into $1/4$-inch slices

1 sweet onion, halved and sliced

2 tablespoons chopped fresh marjoram

Salt and freshly ground black pepper

3 tablespoons olive oil, or 4 tablespoons butter, cut into pieces

$3/4$ cup grated Parmesan cheese, for sprinkling

ROASTED POTATOES with GARLIC and ROSEMARY

SERVES 12 *You can make this simple recipe year round and never grow tired of it. It is excellent for buffets as it can be scaled up or down to feed any number of hungry folk and it goes with every type of meal. Use as much or as little olive oil as you like, just be sure all the potatoes are coated.*

◆ ◆ ◆

Preheat the oven to 400°F. Coat 1 or 2 baking sheets with vegetable oil cooking spray or line them with parchment paper. Toss the potatoes with the garlic, rosemary, and olive oil to coat and arrange them in a single layer on the prepared baking sheets. Bake for 35 to 45 minutes, until a luscious golden brown, stirring once or twice for even browning.

TRANSPORTATION NOTES: Transport fully baked and tightly covered on the baking sheets or in the serving bowl. Or the potatoes can be baked on site: carry the prepared ingredients in large resealable plastic bags and bring baking sheets and parchment paper.

ON SITE/PREPARATION: Do not chill and reheat. Serve warm or at room temperature, or bake on site following the directions above. Transfer the potatoes to the serving bowl and place on the buffet.

Preparation Timeline: Prepare and bake right before serving

Serving Equipment: Serving bowl, serving spoon

On site/Reheat: No

On site/Refrigeration: No

Serving Temperature: Hot or room temperature

3 pounds unpeeled small new potatoes (any variety), halved

5 cloves garlic, pressed or minced

1 1/2 to 2 teaspoons crumbled dried rosemary, or 1 1/2 tablespoons minced fresh rosemary

1/2 cup extra-virgin olive oil

BAKED SAFFRON RICE with ALMONDS and GOLDEN RAISINS

SERVES 12 *Dried fruit and nuts are the perfect complement to saffron rice. Since saffron is a pungent herb with concentrated flavor, only a pinch is needed. This dish goes well with all type of meals, especially shrimp or crab, beef, chicken, and lamb.*

◆ ◆ ◆

Preheat the oven to 350°F. Heat the broth to boiling in a saucepan or in the microwave. Add the saffron and raisins. Set aside.

In a large skillet over medium heat, melt 2 tablespoons of the butter. Add the almonds and cook, stirring often, until golden brown, about 2 minutes (watch carefully: these cook fast and can burn). Transfer to paper towels to drain.

Add the remaining 14 tablespoons butter to the skillet over medium-high heat. Add the onion and sauté until soft, about 5 minutes. Add the rice and stir for a few minutes to coat with butter. Transfer to the casserole and stir in the saffron broth, plumped raisins, and almonds. Cover with the lid or foil and bake in the center of the oven for 1 hour, or until all the liquid is absorbed.

TRANSPORTATION NOTES: Tightly cover and place in a position to prevent tipping.

ON SITE/PREPARATION: Remove the covering, fluff with a fork, and serve warm or at room temperature. To reheat, cover and warm at 350°F for 15 to 45 minutes.

Preparation Timeline: Bake the day of serving

Serving Equipment: Shallow 4-quart casserole or 10 by 10 by 4-inch baking dish, oversize serving spoon

On site/Reheat: Optional

On site/Refrigeration: No

Serving Temperature: Hot, warm, or room temperature

5 cups chicken broth or water

Generous pinch of saffron threads

1 cup golden raisins

16 tablespoons (1 cup) unsalted butter

1 cup blanched slivered almonds

1 yellow or white onion, finely chopped

3 cups basmati rice, long-grain white rice, or converted rice

2 teaspoons salt

Freshly ground black or white pepper

OVEN-FRIED VEGETABLES with MARGARITA DIPPING SAUCE

SERVES 15 *Love deep-fried tempura vegetable chunks but don't like the mess or added fat? Here is one of my favorite easy vegetable dishes for buffet crowds. These chunky vegetables go alongside fancy roasts and casseroles just as well as barbecue or burritos.*

◆ ◆ ◆

To make the dipping sauce, thoroughly combine all the ingredients in a bowl with a whisk or pulse in a food processor. Transfer to a covered container and refrigerate until serving.

To prepare the vegetables, preheat the oven to 425°F. Line 2 or 3 large baking sheets with parchment paper and set aside.

Place the bread crumbs and the cheese in a 1-gallon plastic food bag and shake to combine. Place the vegetables in 1 or 2 bowls. Add the mayonnaise to the vegetables and toss with a spatula until lightly but evenly coated. (The vegetables need to be completely coated for the bread crumbs to stick properly.) Working in batches, place the coated vegetables in the crumb mixture and shake gently to coat well. Arrange the vegetables on the baking sheets in a single layer so they don't touch. Bake for 15 minutes, or until crispy and golden brown. Cool on the baking sheet.

TRANSPORTATION NOTES: Pile the cooled cooked vegetables onto 1 baking sheet or arrange them on the serving platter or basket, tightly cover, and place in a position to prevent tipping. Transport the sauce in the covered container and keep chilled.

ON SITE/PREPARATION: Unwrap the vegetables and arrange them, if necessary. Transfer the dipping sauce to a serving bowl and place next to the vegetables.

Preparation Timeline: **The sauce can be made up to 2 days ahead, if refrigerated; make the vegetables the day of serving**

Serving Equipment: **Platter, lined basket, or Chinese steamer baskets; tongs; bowl and spoon for sauce**

On site/Reheat: **Optional**

On site/Refrigeration: **Sauce only**

Serving Temperature: **Room temperature or warm**

MARGARITA DIPPING SAUCE

3 cups mayonnaise

1/4 cup freshly squeezed lime juice

3 tablespoons orange liqueur (such as Cointreau)

1 tablespoon gold tequila

Few grinds of black pepper

About 3 cups Italian-seasoned dried bread crumbs

1 cup grated Parmesan or Asiago cheese

1 whole broccoli, broken into florets

1 whole cauliflower, broken into florets

1/2 pound fresh green beans, trimmed

1 pound zucchini and/or yellow summer squash, diagonally cut into 1-inch rounds or into 3-inch-long wedges

1 (12-ounce) package defrosted frozen artichoke hearts, drained

3 carrots, diagonally sliced

2 bell peppers (any color), julienned

1/2 pound small whole mushrooms, stemmed

1/4 pound snow peas, strings removed

About 2 cups mayonnaise

ROASTED ASPARAGUS

SERVES 12 *Foolproof and fabulous, roasted asparagus is a hit that everyone seems to love. Don't even bother with a sauce since they taste so good au naturel.*

· · ·

Preheat the oven to 450°F. Divide the asparagus between 2 or 3 baking sheets, spreading them in a single layer. Toss the spears with the olive oil to coat and sprinkle with salt. Bake, uncovered, 1 pan at a time (or switch the position of the pans halfway through). Shake the pan once or twice to turn the asparagus, until they are just tender when pierced with the tip of a sharp knife, about 10 minutes, depending upon thickness.

Transfer to a serving platter, let cool to room temperature, cover, and carry to the party.

TRANSPORTATION NOTES: Tightly cover and place in a position to prevent tipping. If roasting on site, bring the asparagus in a resealable plastic bag and pack olive oil, salt, and baking sheets.

ON SITE/PREPARATION: The asparagus tastes great at room temperature, making it a no-hassle potluck contribution. Simply unwrap and serve. Or if you prefer, roast it on site, following the directions above, and serve warm.

Preparation Timeline: Roast the day of serving, if serving warm, or the day before, if serving cold

Serving Equipment: Platter, serving tongs

On site/Reheat: No

On site/Refrigeration: No

Serving Temperature: Warm, room temperature, or chilled

3 pounds medium-thick stalks asparagus, ends snapped off

1/2 cup olive oil

Salt, for sprinkling

TAMAL AZTECA

SERVES 12 *Tamal Azteca is similar to an enchilada but simpler. This version—from Jeanne Jones, who was inspired by a meal created by Rick Bayless—reminds me how Mexican cooks carefully cultivate flavors.*

◆ ◆ ◆

To make the sauce, purée the tomatoes and chiles in a food processor. In a skillet over medium heat, heat the oil and cook the onion 5 minutes, until soft. Add the garlic and cook 1 minute, until golden. Add the tomatoes and cook, stirring frequently, for 15 minutes, or until the sauce thickens. Add the broth, decrease the heat to low, and simmer, uncovered, for 30 minutes, stirring occasionally. Remove from the heat and stir in the salt and cilantro. (If making the sauce ahead, transfer to a covered container and refrigerate for up to 1 day.)

Preheat the oven to 350°F. Spray 2 baking sheets with oil. Spread the tortillas out on the baking sheets and lightly spray them as well. Bake for 10 minutes, until golden, and then turn and bake for 3 minutes more. Set aside. Leave the oven on, if baking the casserole immediately.

Lightly spray the casserole dish with oil. Spread 1 cup of sauce over the bottom. Cover with 4 tortillas, the spinach, and 1 cup each of the sauce and Jack cheese. Layer with 4 more tortillas, press down, then top with the corn and 1 cup each of the sauce and Jack cheese. Layer 4 more tortillas, press down, sprinkle with the zucchini and 1 cup each of the sauce and Jack cheese. Top with the remaining tortillas, press down, spread the remaining sauce and Jack cheese, and top with the Parmesan. Cover the casserole with foil. (If preparing ahead, the casserole can be refrigerated at this point for up to 12 hours.)

Bake the casserole, covered, for 30 minutes. (If baking a refrigerated casserole, add another 15 minutes.) Remove the foil and bake for another 15 minutes, or until lightly browned and bubbly. Do not overbake, as the tortillas will disintegrate. Cool and cover with foil to transport. Leave at room temperature up to an hour, then refrigerate.

TRANSPORTATION NOTES: Cover and place to prevent tipping.

ON SITE/PREPARATION: Reheat at 350°F, covered, for 20 minutes, or until warmed through. Top with the cilantro and serve.

Preparation Timeline: The sauce can be made up to 1 day ahead and the casserole can be assembled up to 12 hours ahead, if refrigerated

Serving Equipment: 5-quart or 10 by 15 by 2-inch casserole dish, serving spatula

On site/Reheat: Yes

On site/Refrigeration: No

Serving Temperature: Hot or warm

CILANTRO-TOMATO SAUCE

2 (28-ounce) cans plum tomatoes, undrained

2 (4-ounce) cans roasted green chiles, undrained and chopped

2 tablespoons olive oil

1 large white onion, chopped

2 cloves garlic, minced

2 cups chicken broth

1 teaspoon salt

1/2 cup chopped cilantro

16 corn tortillas

4 (10-ounce) packages frozen chopped spinach, thawed and drained well

1 pound Monterey Jack cheese, grated

2 (10-ounce) packages frozen baby white corn, thawed

3 zucchini, stemmed and diced

2/3 cup grated Parmesan cheese or queso asadero

1/2 cup chopped cilantro

CASUAL SUMMER DISHES

COLD ROAST FILET of BEEF with GREEN PEPPERCORN–MUSTARD SAUCE

SERVES 36 *Filet of beef, one of the most tender and coveted of meats, exemplifies elegant dining, but this dish is no trouble to prepare or serve. The green peppercorns, brined under-ripe whole peppercorns, are available canned and have a fresh flavor that adds considerable zing to the sauce.*

◆ ◆ ◆

To make the sauce, combine all the ingredients in a bowl with a whisk. Transfer to a covered container and refrigerate for up to 2 days.

Preheat the oven to 425°F. Place 2 roasting pans near your stove. In a large sauté pan over high heat, melt 1 tablespoon of the butter. Add 1 filet and sear, turning, until it is browned all over the surface, about 5 minutes. Place lengthwise in 1 of the roasting pans. Repeat with the remaining butter and filets, placing 2 in each roasting pan with plenty of room in between. Season each filet with salt and pepper.

Place the pans in the oven and roast 20 minutes for rare. Remove 1 pan and let the second pan roast an additional 5 minutes, for medium, so your guests will have a choice of doneness. Cool the roasts to room temperature, wrap in plastic wrap, then foil, and chill in the refrigerator overnight, if desired.

Carve the cooled roasts into thin slices slightly on the diagonal and arrange on a serving platter. Tightly cover.

TRANSPORTATION NOTES: Tightly cover and place in a position to prevent tipping. Bring the sauce in the covered container and keep cold.

ON SITE/PREPARATION: Slice and arrange the meat, if not done ahead, and place the sauce in a serving bowl. Serve chilled or at room temperature.

Preparation Timeline: The sauce should be prepared and refrigerated 1 to 2 days ahead to allow the flavors to meld; the filet can be made up to 1 day ahead, if refrigerated

Serving Equipment: Large platter, fork, bowl and serving spoon for the sauce

On site/Reheat: No

On site/Refrigeration: Optional for meat; yes for sauce

Serving Temperature: Chilled or cool room temperature

GREEN PEPPERCORN–MUSTARD SAUCE

3 cups mayonnaise

3 cups sour cream

1 cup Dijon mustard

1/2 cup minced fresh flat-leaf parsley

5 tablespoons green peppercorns, drained

4 tablespoons (1/4 cup) butter

4 (41/2-pound) beef tenderloins, trimmed of excess fat and sinew

Salt and freshly ground black pepper

ROASTED RED PEPPERS with GARLIC and PARSLEY

SERVES 12 TO 15 *You will always be popular at a potluck if you show up with a big platter of roasted peppers marinated in their own juices. I once heard these described at a potluck as "the caviar of peppers." They are excellent served with sliced fresh crusty French bread.*

◆ ◆ ◆

Preheat the broiler. Place the peppers on a baking sheet and broil, turning often with tongs, until the skins blister and are completely charred, about 13 minutes. Immediately place the peppers in a paper or plastic bag. Close the bag and let the peppers cool to room temperature, about 20 minutes (the steam will loosen the charred skin). Cut open 1 side of each cooled pepper and pull out and discard the seeds, ribs, and stem. With a paring knife, peel the peppers over a small bowl, to collect the juices. Discard the skins. If some of the skin sticks, rinse it under cold water. (If making ahead, the peppers can be refrigerated in their juices, covered, for up to 3 days.)

Cut each pepper in half and then into 2 or 3 pieces. Arrange the pieces on the serving platter in a single layer or slightly overlapping. Drizzle with the oil, then sprinkle with the garlic, parsley, and any collected juices. Cover with plastic wrap and refrigerate for up to 1 day.

TRANSPORTATION NOTES: Tightly cover and place in a position to prevent tipping.

ON SITE/PREPARATION: Unwrap the dish and serve.

Preparation Timeline: Best made 1 day ahead and refrigerated overnight

Serving Equipment: Large serving platter or large gratin dish (if serving warm), serving fork

On site/Reheat: Optional

On site/Refrigeration: No

Serving Temperature: Chilled, room temperature, or warm

8 large red bell peppers

About 1/2 cup extra-virgin or light olive oil

4 to 6 cloves garlic, minced

1/2 bunch fresh flat-leaf parsley, finely chopped

COLD BAKED CHICKEN BREASTS
with JALAPEÑO PLUM SAUCE

SERVES 12 *A platter of cold chicken glazed with barbecue sauce is always a welcome sight on a buffet table. Here the boneless skinless breasts, which you can buy in big bags from the frozen food aisle for crowds, are conveniently baked instead of grilled outside. The jalapeño plum sauce is a nice change from more ubiquitous barbecue sauces.*

◆ ◆ ◆

To make the sauce, purée the canned plums with their syrup in a food processor (or dice the fresh plums). Heat the oil over medium-high heat in a saucepan. Add the onion, garlic, and jalapeño and sauté until tender, about 5 minutes. Add the plums, curry powder, allspice, honey, chile sauce, lemon juice, soy sauce, and marmalade and bring to a simmer. Decrease the heat to low and cook for about 1 1/2 hours, stirring often, until thick. Remove from the heat and cool to room temperature. With an immersion blender or in a food processor, purée the sauce a little, leaving some chunks. (If making ahead, transfer to a covered container and refrigerate for up to 2 weeks, or freeze for up to 1 month.)

Preheat the oven to 400°F. Line an 11 by 17-inch rimmed baking sheet with heavy-duty aluminum foil, making a rim to avoid leaks. Brush both sides of each breast liberally with the plum sauce and arrange the pieces in a single layer on the baking sheet. Bake until the breasts are no longer pink inside, about 20 minutes. Cool for 30 minutes and then transfer to a deep casserole, cover, and transport immediately (or if making in advance, the chicken can be refrigerated for up to 1 day).

TRANSPORTATION NOTES: Tightly cover and place in a position to prevent tipping.

ON SITE/PREPARATION: To serve, cut each breast crosswise into 3 or 4 sections and place on the serving platter. Serve any extra plum sauce on the side.

Preparation Timeline: **The sauce can be made up to 2 weeks ahead, if refrigerated; the chicken can be baked up to 1 day ahead, if refrigerated**

Serving Equipment: **Serving platter, knife, serving fork or tongs**

On site/Reheat: **No**

On site/Refrigeration: **Optional**

Serving Temperature: **Room temperature or chilled**

JALAPEÑO PLUM SAUCE

2 (16-ounce) cans whole purple plums in syrup, or 2 1/2 pounds fresh plums, pitted

5 tablespoons olive oil

1 yellow onion, minced

2 cloves garlic, minced

1 jalapeño chile, seeds and ribs removed, minced

1 tablespoon curry powder

1 teaspoon ground allspice

3/4 cup honey

1/2 cup tomato-chile sauce

1/3 cup freshly squeezed lemon juice

1/3 cup soy sauce

1/4 cup orange marmalade

12 (5- to 6-ounce) boneless skinless chicken breasts, rinsed and patted dry

BAKED CHICKEN TENDERS with CREOLE MUSTARD SAUCE

SERVES 12 *Before you say you will never make a recipe that uses a kid's breakfast cereal, I ask you to consider. Based on southern fried chicken recipes and updated for the low-fat crowd, this fantastic recipe is adapted from one served at Planet Hollywood restaurants. The oven-fried chicken tenders are perfect for a buffet with young people in attendance.*

◆ ◆ ◆

To make the mustard sauce, thoroughly combine all of the sauce ingredients in a bowl with a whisk or pulse in a food processor. Transfer to a covered container and refrigerate until serving, up to 2 days.

Preheat the oven to 375°F. Line 2 large rimmed baking sheets with foil. In a food processor, coarsely grind the Cap'n Crunch and corn flakes. Transfer to a shallow bowl. In another shallow bowl, beat the eggs with the milk. In a third shallow bowl or in a small brown paper bag, mix the flour, onion powder, garlic powder, and pepper.

Dip the chicken pieces into the seasoned flour, coating well and shaking off any excess flour, or shake them in the paper bag. Dip the chicken into the egg mixure, coating well and letting the excess drip off, and then dip into the cereal mixture to coat well. Place the pieces on the baking sheets in a single layer and lightly spray with oil cooking spray. Bake for 15 to 18 minutes, or until the tenders are golden on the outside and the meat is no longer pink inside.

Preparation Timeline: The sauce can be made up to 2 days ahead and the chicken tenders can be baked 4 to 6 hours in advance, if refrigerated

Serving Equipment: Large platter, fork or tongs, bowl and serving spoon for the sauce

On site/Reheat: Optional

On site/Refrigeration: Optional for meat; yes for sauce

Serving Temperature: Hot, warm, or room temperature

CREOLE MUSTARD SAUCE

2 cups mayonnaise

$3/4$ block silken tofu, or $1/2$ cup mayonnaise

$1/2$ cup Creole-style or Dijon mustard

2 tablespoons yellow mustard

2 tablespoons horseradish

2 teaspoons apple cider vinegar

2 teaspoons red wine vinegar

2 teaspoons water

2 dashes Worcestershire sauce

$1/4$ teaspoon cayenne pepper

6 green onions, white and some of the green parts, thinly sliced

1 clove garlic, crushed

2 tablespoons minced green bell pepper

2 tablespoons minced celery

1 shallot, minced

TRANSPORTATION NOTES: Pack the tenders in plastic refrigerator bags or place on a platter and tightly cover to transport. Carry the sauce in a covered container and keep chilled. Bring a baking sheet, if you plan to reheat on site.

ON SITE/PREPARATION: Serve warm or at room temperature, or reheat the tenders at 350°F for 5 minutes, until heated through. Arrange on a platter and place the sauce in the serving bowl.

3 heaping cups Cap'n Crunch cereal

2^1/$_2$ cups corn flakes

2 large eggs

1^1/$_2$ cups milk

1^1/$_2$ cups all-purpose flour

1^1/$_2$ teaspoons onion powder

1^1/$_2$ teaspoons garlic powder

Few grinds of black pepper

3 pounds chicken breasts, cut into 1-ounce tenders, or frozen chicken tenders, thawed

Olive oil cooking spray

ZUCCHINI and OLIVE ENCHILADAS

SERVES 12 *My mother has been making these delightfully unique vege-tarian enchiladas as long as I can remember. I think the recipe might have even come from* Sunset *magazine a few decades ago. This casse-role cannot be frozen before cooking because the fresh zucchini will become too watery and the tortillas will disintegrate, so make it the day you are going to eat it.*

• • •

To make the sauce, heat the olive oil in a 3-quart pan over medium heat. Add the onion and peppers and sauté until soft, about 10 minutes. Add the remaining sauce ingredients and stir to combine. Simmer for 30 minutes, until thickened, stirring occasionally. Remove the bay leaf. (If making ahead, cool and refrigerate. Then just before assembling the enchiladas, warm over medium heat until hot.)

To assemble the enchiladas, place the casserole dishes by your work surface. Dip 1 tortilla in the hot tomato sauce for up to 1 minute to soften it. Put the tortilla on a plate and place a heaping 1/2 cup of the grated zucchini, a few sliced olives, and 3 tablespoons of cheese in the middle. Roll the tortilla up and place it seam-side down in 1 of the casseroles. Repeat to fill the remaining tortillas, laying them side by side in the casseroles. Pour the sauce over the tortillas and sprinkle the top with the remaining cheese. (If making ahead, the enchiladas can be covered and refrigerated at this point, up to 12 hours. Allow the casseroles to return to room temperature before baking, about 1 hour.)

Preheat the oven to 350°F. Bake, uncovered, for 30 to 40 minutes, until bubbling hot. Serve hot from the oven or warm. Or cool to room temperature, cover, refrigerate, and reheat on site.

continued

Preparation Timeline: The sauce can be made up to 2 days ahead and the enchiladas can be assembled up to 12 hours ahead, if refrigerated

Serving Equipment: Two 3-quart oval or 9 by 13-inch casserole dishes, serving spatula

On site/Reheat: Optional

On site/Refrigeration: No

Serving Temperature: Hot or warm

CHUNKY TOMATO AND BELL PEPPER SAUCE

1/4 cup olive oil

1 large yellow onion, chopped

2 bell peppers (any color), coarsely chopped

2 cloves garlic, minced or pressed

2 (15-ounce) cans tomato sauce

2 (16-ounce) cans whole tomatoes in juice, broken up

1 bay leaf

2 scant tablespoons chili powder

2 teaspoons dried marjoram

2 teaspoons sugar

1 teaspoon dried basil

1 teaspoon ground cumin

1/3 teaspoon cayenne pepper

Pinch of salt

TRANSPORTATION NOTES: Bring the sour cream and cilantro in separate covered containers or wrapped small serving bowls. Tightly cover the casseroles with foil and place them on the floor of the car or in the trunk with a large thick towel wrapped around the base to prevent tipping, or place in an insulated cooler for longer transport.

ON SITE/PREPARATION: Serve warm or hot. Reheat, if necessary, uncovered, at 350°F for 10 minutes. To bake on site, bring the chilled, uncooked casseroles to room temperature before baking according to the directions above. Place the sour cream and chopped cilantro in serving bowls and serve on the side.

24 fresh yellow or white corn tortillas

3 pounds zucchini, coarsely shredded

2 (2^1/$_2$-ounce) cans sliced black olives

8 cups (about 2 pounds) shredded Cheddar cheese or mixture of Cheddar and Monterey Jack

1 pint sour cream, for garnish (optional)

^{1}/$_2$ cup minced cilantro, for garnish

ROASTED EGGPLANT, TOMATO, and MOZZARELLA CASSEROLE

SERVES 8 *This casserole is a simpler relative of eggplant Parmesan, with roasted eggplant instead of fried. You can use the Italian, baby purple, or white eggplant in place of the more common globe eggplant for this dish, but all need to be salted first to remove the bitterness.*

• • •

Sprinkle both sides of the eggplant with salt and layer between double layers of paper towels. Let stand 15 minutes.

Preheat the oven to 450°F. Line a large baking sheet with parchment paper and brush with olive oil. Discard the paper towels and place the eggplant on the baking sheet. Roast for 10 minutes, turning once, until soft and browned. Remove from the oven and decrease the heat to 350°F (unless you are preparing the casserole in advance). In a small bowl, combine the ricotta, eggs, basil, and half of the Parmesan.

Place 1/2 cup of the tomato sauce on the bottom of the baking dish. Layer with one-third of the eggplant in overlapping slices, one-third of the mozzarella, and half of the ricotta mixture. Drizzle with 2 cups of the tomato sauce. Repeat, ending with a layer of eggplant. Top with the remaining tomato sauce. Sprinkle with the remaining Parmesan and the mozzarella. (The casserole can be covered and refrigerated at this point. Allow it to return to room temperature before baking.)

Bake, uncovered, for 45 to 50 minutes, until bubbling hot. Let stand for a few minutes before cutting.

TRANSPORTATION NOTES: Cover tightly with foil and place the casseroles on the floor of the car or in the trunk with a large thick towel wrapped around the base to prevent tipping.

ON SITE/PREPARATION: Serve warm or at room temperature. To reheat, bake uncovered at 350°F for 15 minutes, or until warmed through. To bake on site, allow the chilled uncooked casserole to return to room temperature before baking according to the directions above. Serve immediately.

Preparation Timeline: Can be made up to 1 day ahead, if refrigerated

Serving Equipment: 9 by 13-inch or 10 by 14-inch baking dish, oversize serving spoon

On site/Reheat: Optional

On site/Refrigeration: No

Serving Temperature: Hot, warm, or room temperature

4 pounds eggplant, peeled or unpeeled and cut into 1/4-inch slices

1 tablespoon salt

1 (15-ounce) container whole milk ricotta cheese

2 large eggs

2 heaping tablespoons minced fresh basil

3/4 cup shredded Parmesan cheese

5 cups canned plain tomato sauce

2 (12-ounce) whole milk mozzarella balls, sliced

VEGETABLE TORTA with FRESH BASIL

SERVES 8 (MAKES ONE 10-INCH TORTA) *Baked in a springform pan and served in wedges like a cake, this thick vegetable torta is one of my favorite dishes to make for gatherings since it is best made the day before and reheated. I have made literally dozens of these at a time for catering buffets, and it is always a hit as a side dish at barbecues.*

+ + +

Preheat the oven to 350°F, if baking immediately. Brush the bottom and sides of a 10-inch springform pan with oil. To prevent leaking, wrap the outside of the pan with a sheet of aluminum foil.

In a large skillet, heat the olive oil over medium heat. Add the onion, mushrooms, zucchini, yellow squash, and peppers and sauté until crisp-tender, stirring occasionally, about 15 minutes. While the vegetables are cooking, whisk together the eggs, half-and-half, and basil in a large bowl and season with salt and pepper. Stir in the bread cubes and the cheeses.

Add the sautéed vegetables to the bread mixture and stir with a large rubber spatula to combine. Transfer to the prepared pan and pack the mixture tightly. Place the pan on a baking sheet.

Bake for about 1 hour, until firm to the touch, puffed, and golden brown. Serve warm or cool to room temperature, cover, and refrigerate.

TRANSPORTATION NOTES:: Tightly cover and place in a position to prevent tipping.

ON SITE/PREPARATION: Reheat, if desired, at 350°F for 15 minutes, or until warmed through. To serve, cut into pie-shaped wedges.

Preparation Timeline: **Best made 1 to 2 days ahead, if refrigerated**

Serving Equipment: **Round serving platter, sharp knife, triangular pie server (or a large serving platter and serving spatula, if serving presliced wedges)**

On site/Reheat: **Optional**

On site/Refrigeration: **Optional**

Serving Temperature: **Hot, room temperature, or cold**

1/4 cup olive oil

1 large yellow onion, chopped

8 ounces fresh mushrooms, cleaned and sliced

3 zucchini, sliced 1/4 inch thick

3 yellow summer squash, sliced 1/4 inch thick

1 red bell pepper, cut into 1/4-inch-thick strips

1 yellow bell pepper, cut into 1/4-inch-thick strips

6 large eggs

1/4 cup half-and-half or evaporated milk

3 tablespoons chopped fresh basil

Salt and freshly ground black pepper

About 3 cups day-old bread, in 1/2-inch cubes

1 (8-ounce) package cream cheese, cut into chunks

2 cups (6 to 8 ounces) shredded Jarlsberg or Swiss cheese

MAQUE CHOUX

SERVES 8 *If you are familiar with Creole cooking, you know about maque choux—the corn, pepper, and tomato preparation that is one of the flavor foundations of the cuisine. While you can make this dish with canned tomatoes and frozen corn in the winter, it is best served in the summer, when fresh corn and tomatoes are at their peak.*

◆ ◆ ◆

In a large skillet, melt the butter over medium heat. Add the onion, bell pepper, jalapeño if desired, and garlic and sauté for about 10 minutes, until the onion is translucent. Stir in the corn and tomatoes with their juices and cook for 5 more minutes, stirring occasionally. Add the broth and season with the cayenne, salt, pepper, and Tabasco. Decrease the heat to medium-low and partially cover. Cook until all the liquid is absorbed, about 45 minutes, stirring occasionally. Place in a serving bowl and cover. Can stand for a few hours at room temperature until transporting.

    TRANSPORTATION NOTES: Tightly cover and place in a position to prevent tipping.

    ON SITE/PREPARATION: Unwrap and serve.

Preparation Timeline: Best made the day of serving, 1 to 4 hours ahead

Serving Equipment: Serving bowl, large serving spoon

On site/Reheat: No

On site/Refrigeration: No

Serving Temperature: Warm or room temperature

1 stick ($1/2$ cup) unsalted butter, or $1/4$ cup olive oil

1 yellow onion, finely chopped

1 large green bell pepper, seeded and finely chopped

1 jalapeño chile, finely chopped (optional)

1 large clove garlic, finely chopped

Kernels from 8 to 9 ears corn ($4^1/2$ to 5 cups)

2 medium-large ripe tomatoes, peeled, seeded, and chopped

1 cup canned low-sodium chicken broth

$1/8$ teaspoon cayenne pepper

A pinch of salt and freshly ground black pepper

Dash of Tabasco sauce

CALICO BEAN BAKE

SERVES 10 *I have no idea when or where the term "calico" became part of these baked beans, but perhaps it is because there is a mixture of beans and the resulting dish looks a bit speckled. I got the recipe from my boyfriend's mother in the 1970s and brought it to a summer barbecue with my family. It was an instant hit and now even my mom makes it as well. It has become a staple at our barbecues and potluck buffets. These beans are fantastic the next day cold.*

• • •

Preheat the oven to 350°F. Melt the butter in a small skillet over medium heat. Add the onion and sauté until soft, about 5 minutes. Add the garlic and cook for 30 seconds, until limp. Combine all the beans in a bowl and add the ketchup, brown sugar, vinegar, and mustard. Add the onion and garlic and stir to combine. Transfer to a deep ceramic casserole and lay the bacon strips over the top, pressing into the beans.

Bake, uncovered, for 1 hour, then decrease the oven temperature to 300°F and bake another 1 to 1½ hours, until hot and bubbly.

TRANSPORTATION NOTES: Tightly cover and place in a position to prevent tipping.

ON SITE/PREPARATION: Reheat, if desired, at 350°F for 20 minutes. Also good at room temperature.

Preparation Timeline: Can be made up to 1 day ahead, if refrigerated

Serving Equipment: 3-quart oval or round casserole dish, serving spoon

On site/Reheat: Optional

On site/Refrigeration: No

Serving Temperature: Hot, warm, or room temperature

1 tablespoon butter

1 large yellow onion, finely chopped

1 clove garlic, minced

1 (32-ounce) can brick-oven-baked pork and beans

1 (16-ounce) can kidney beans, drained and rinsed

1 (15½-ounce) can butter beans, drained and rinsed

1 (16-ounce) can garbanzo beans, drained and rinsed

¾ cup ketchup

3 tablespoons light or dark brown sugar

3 tablespoons apple cider vinegar

2 teaspoons Dijon mustard

6 slices lean smoky bacon

PASTA with TWO PESTOS

SERVES 8 *While basil pesto is common, now there are pestos made with spinach, cilantro, parsley, tomatoes, and all manner of nuts. This one, made with sundried tomatoes, happens to be a favorite of mine and is a delightful flavor revelation if you have not made it before. I have doubled and tripled this recipe with no problem, and it looks stunning on a large oval platter. This recipe is adapted from one created by one of my first cooking mentors, food writer Louise Fiszer, a consummate home entertainer.*

◆ ◆ ◆

The steps for making the pestos are the same. Make each separately: first, add the garlic to the bowl of a food processor and finely chop. Add the rest of the pesto ingredients, except the oil. Pulse while slowly adding the oil, to form a slightly coarse purée. The pestos may also be made by hand using a mortar and pestle or in a blender. Store the pestos, covered, in the refrigerator until ready to use. (If making the day before, pour a thin layer of olive oil over each pesto to seal it and keep it fresh. Pestos can also be frozen up to 1 month.)

Bring the pestos to room temperature while you cook the pasta according to the package instructions. Drain the pasta in a colander and lightly toss with the olive oil to prevent sticking. Place the pasta on the serving platter and toss with the basil pesto until evenly distributed. Spoon the sundried tomato pesto around the top in a circle. Garnish with the basil leaves if desired.

TRANSPORTATION NOTES: Tightly cover and place in a position to prevent tipping.

ON SITE/PREPARATION: Simply unwrap and serve.

Preparation Timeline: **The pestos can be made up to 2 days ahead, if refrigerated, or 1 month, if frozen; the pasta can be made up to 2 hours before serving**

Serving Equipment: **Serving platter with a shallow rim, serving spoon, fork or tongs**

On site/Reheat: **No**

On site/Refrigeration: **No**

Serving Temperature: **Warm or room temperature**

SUNDRIED TOMATO PESTO

1 clove garlic, peeled

3 ounces ($1/3$ cup) dry-packed sundried tomatoes, soaked in hot water for 1 hour and drained

$1/4$ cup grated Parmesan cheese

$1/4$ bunch fresh flat-leaf parsley, stemmed

3 tablespoons tomato paste

$1/4$ to $1/2$ cup olive oil

BASIL PESTO

2 cloves garlic, peeled

$2 1/2$ cups fresh basil leaves

$1/2$ cup grated Parmesan cheese

$1/4$ cup pine nuts

$1/3$ to $1/2$ cup olive oil

$1 1/2$ pounds fresh or dried fettuccine (regular or whole wheat)

4 to 6 tablespoons olive oil

Basil leaves, for garnish (optional)

GREEN CHILE and RICE CASSEROLE

SERVES 12 *Rice is layered with green chiles and cheese in this delicious, homey, baked Mexican side dish. I have made this many times to bring to buffets, especially when I am short on time. It is so popular, there is never any left, so I make enough to allow half the guests, including myself, to have a second helping.*

◆ ◆ ◆

Preheat the oven to 350°F, if baking immediately. Brush the casserole with butter or olive oil. In a bowl, mix the sour cream, salt, and green chiles, stirring to combine evenly.

Place a third of the rice in the prepared casserole, then cover with half of the sour cream mixture and half of the cheese strips. Repeat the layers, ending with a layer of rice, smoothed to the edges. Top with the Cheddar cheese and cover with foil. (If making ahead, the casserole can be refrigerated at this point, covered, up to 1 day.)

Bake, covered, for 1 to 1¼ hours, until bubbling hot and browned around the edges.

TRANSPORTATION NOTES: Tightly cover and place in a position to prevent tipping.

ON SITE/PREPARATION: Serve at room temperature or reheat, covered, at 350°F for 15 minutes, until warmed through.

Preparation Timeline: Can be made up to 1 day ahead, if refrigerated

Serving Equipment: 3-quart oval or 9 by 13-inch casserole dish, serving spoon

On site/Reheat: Optional

On site/Refrigeration: No

Serving Temperature: Hot, warm, or room temperature

3 pints sour cream

1 teaspoon salt

2 (7-ounce) cans diced roasted green chiles, drained

6 cups cooked long-grain white or brown rice

1½ pounds Monterey Jack, Muenster, or fontina cheese, cut into ½-inch strips

4 ounces Cheddar cheese, shredded (about 1 cup), or 1 cup grated Parmesan cheese

FESTIVE AUTUMN FEASTS

MUSHROOM LASAGNA

SERVES 8 *Here is a gourmet's delight of a lasagna. Look for the dried porcini mushrooms in the produce section of the supermarket or in a specialty foods store; they add an earthy quality that cannot be duplicated with just fresh mushrooms.*

◆ ◆ ◆

To make the mushroom sauce, cover the dried mushrooms with the boiling water in a small bowl; let stand for 30 minutes.

In a deep heavy saucepan, heat the oil over medium-high heat. Add the onion, carrot, and celery and sauté until tender but not browned, 2 to 3 minutes. Add the shiitake mushrooms, tomato purée, garlic, and salt and bring to a boil over high heat, stirring constantly. Drain and rinse the porcinis, discarding the liquid, and then add them to the tomato sauce. Decrease the heat to low and cook, uncovered, for 45 minutes to 1 hour, stirring occasionally. Cool to room temperature (or cover and refrigerate up to 1 day).

To make the white sauce, melt the butter in a heavy saucepan over medium heat. Stir in the flour, salt, and nutmeg and cook until bubbly. With a whisk, gradually stir in the milk. Heat to boiling, stirring constantly, until thickened and smooth. Cool to room temperature (or cover and refrigerate up to 1 day).

Spray a large piece of foil with vegetable oil cooking spray. Soak the fresh lasagna noodles in boiling water for 3 minutes to soften (or 10 minutes, if using dried noodles). Drain the noodles and place them in a single layer on the foil to prevent sticking. Cut them, if needed, to fit your baking dish.

To assemble the lasagna, heavily butter the bottom of the baking dish. Preheat the oven to 375°F, if baking immediately. Spread half of the mushroom sauce over the bottom of the dish, then add 1 layer of the pasta, half of the white sauce, another layer of pasta, half of both cheeses, another layer of pasta, then repeat, ending with the cheeses. (If making ahead, the casserole can be covered with foil and refrigerated up to 1 day.)

continued

Preparation Timeline: **The sauces and the lasagna can be prepared up to 1 day ahead, if refrigerated**

Serving Equipment: **3-quart or 9 by 1 3-inch casserole dish, serving spatula**

On site/Reheat: **Yes**

On site/Refrigeration: **No**

Serving Temperature: **Hot or warm**

MUSHROOM SAUCE

1 ounce dried porcini mushrooms

$1/2$ cup boiling water

3 tablespoons olive oil

1 medium-small yellow onion, finely chopped

1 carrot, finely chopped

1 rib celery, finely chopped

3 pounds fresh shiitake mushrooms, cleaned and coarsely chopped

1 (29-ounce) can tomato purée

2 cloves garlic, minced or pressed

1 teaspoon salt

ITALIAN WHITE SAUCE

5 tablespoons ($1/3$ cup) unsalted butter

$1/3$ cup all-purpose flour

$1/4$ teaspoon salt

$1/8$ teaspoon ground nutmeg

$1^1/2$ cups milk

Bake, covered, for 45 minutes, or until hot, bubbly, and golden brown. Allow the casserole to cool until it can be safely handled and then transport.

TRANSPORTATION NOTES: Cover the casserole tightly in foil and place it on the floor of the car or in the trunk with a large thick towel wrapped around the base to prevent tipping, or place it in an insulated cooler for longer transport.

ON SITE/PREPARATION: To reheat, bake at 350°F, covered, for 25 to 40 minutes, until warmed in the center.

5 sheets fresh lasagna noodles, or 12 ounces dried lasagna noodles

1 1-pound ball fresh mozzarella cheese, thinly sliced

3/4 cup shredded or grated Parmesan cheese

GLAZED CORNISH GAME HENS

SERVES 12 *Cornish game hens, once a specialty item, are easily available in butcher shops or in the freezer section of most supermarkets. They are fantastic and I have made them many times for large parties where the guests can sit down, use a knife and fork, and gnaw on the leg if they are so inclined. This recipe is a nice menu choice for a Thanksgiving buffet in lieu of turkey or for a late-summer outdoor picnic.*

◆ ◆ ◆

Preheat the oven to 400°F. Rinse the game hens inside and out with cold water and pat dry. To split each game hen, place the bird breast side up on a cutting surface. Holding the bird with 1 hand and using kitchen shears with the other, cut the breast in half, starting from the neck. Turn the bird over and cut down both sides of the backbone, as close as possible, leaving two halves; discard the backbone, or freeze for making soup stock. Season the hen halves inside and out with the salt and pepper. Place them side by side in a roasting pan.

Combine the marmalade and liqueur in a small saucepan and mix with a fork. Heat gently over medium heat just to melt. Pour half the glaze over the hens with a large spoon or brush to coat evenly.

Place the roasting pan in the oven, decrease the temperature to 350°F, and roast for 30 minutes. Remove the pan from the oven, pour the remaining glaze over the hens, and then return the pan to the oven to roast for 1 more hour, until the hens are browned and the juices run clear. Let cool for 30 minutes and then arrange the halves on the serving platter and cover tightly. Transport warm or refrigerate until transporting.

TRANSPORTATION NOTES: Tightly cover and place in a position to prevent tipping.

ON SITE/PREPARATION: If you are serving the prebaked hens cold, allow them to return to a cool room temperature before serving. Serve immediately and garnish with the grape clusters.

Preparation Timeline: Roast the day of serving

Serving Equipment: Large platter, serving fork

On site/Reheat: No

On site/Refrigeration: Optional

Serving Temperature: Warm or cool room temperature

6 (1½- to 1¾-pound) Cornish game hens

Salt and freshly ground black pepper

3 cups orange marmalade, quince jelly, or apricot preserves

⅓ cup orange liqueur

1 pound Ribier grapes, for garnish

ROLLED STUFFED TURKEY BREAST
with PROSCIUTTO and PROVOLONE

SERVES 16 *This is a wonderful alternative to preparing a whole stuffed bird for a Thanksgiving buffet. Boned turkey breast roasts are readily available at butcher shops. They roast up tender and juicy, are incredibly easy to assemble, and are not messy to serve. Since both the ham and the cheese are salty, I don't worry about seasoning inside.*

◆ ◆ ◆

On a flat surface, place one of the breasts boned-side up. Butterfly the breast to make the meat an even thickness: slice the breast in half horizontally, but do not cut all the way through. Leave 1 side attached and open the meat like a book. Using half of the prosciutto, cover the meat surface with overlapping slices. Arrange half of the cheese over the prosciutto and cover with half of the spinach. Starting at the short end, roll the roast up in a jelly-roll fashion into a cylinder and tie in 3 places with kitchen twine to secure. Arrange the turkey breast seam-side down in a roasting pan. Repeat with the other breast. Cover with foil. (If making ahead, the turkey can be refrigerated at this point for up to 1 day before roasting.)

Preheat the oven to 350°F. Rub the turkey with the olive oil. Roast for 1 hour to 1 hour 20 minutes (20 to 25 minutes per pound), until an instant-read thermometer inserted into the thickest part of the meat reads 160°F and the juices run clear. Let rest, covered with foil, for at least 30 minutes before carving, if serving warm.

The turkey can be carved at home or on site. To carve on site, tightly wrap in foil and refrigerate until transporting. If carving at home, uncover the turkey, remove the strings, cut into 1-inch-thick slices, and arrange them on the serving platter. Tightly cover the platter and transport immediately or refrigerate up to 8 hours, to serve cold.

TRANSPORTATION NOTES: Transport the baked turkey wrapped tightly either whole or arranged on the serving platter. Bring a knife and cutting board, if carving on site.

ON SITE/PREPARATION: Unwrap the platter and place on the buffet or carve the meat on site.

Preparation Timeline: **Can be prepared and/or roasted up to 1 day ahead, if refrigerated**

Serving Equipment: **Large platter, serving fork**

On site/Reheat: **No**

On site/Refrigeration: **Optional**

Serving Temperature: **Warm or room temperature**

---

2 (4- to 5-pound) boneless turkey breast halves with skin, rinsed and patted dry, netting removed

4 ounces paper-thin slices prosciutto

10 slices provolone cheese

10 to 14 whole leaves fresh spinach, stemmed

3 tablespoons olive oil

OLD-FASHIONED BEEF and ANASAZI BEAN CHILI

SERVES 15 *Sometimes you need a good chili, not overpoweringly hot, for a buffet crowd. Native to the American Southwest, Anasazi beans are probably an updated strain from beans grown long ago. They are speckled like pintos but a cranberry color instead of pinkish brown.*

◆ ◆ ◆

To make the chili spice bag, wrap the red pepper flakes, cloves, cumin seeds, oregano, and bay leaf in a small square of cheesecloth and tie with kitchen twine.

Heat 3 tablespoons of the olive oil in a very large skillet over medium-high heat. Working in batches if necessary, cook the ground beef and garlic until the meat is browned, about 8 minutes; drain off the fat.

Meanwhile, heat the remaining 3 tablespoons olive oil in a Dutch oven over medium-high heat. Add the onions and bell peppers and sauté until soft, about 4 minutes. Add the undrained tomatoes, tomato paste, beer, chili powder, jalapeño, and the spice bag; stir to combine and mash the tomatoes. Add the beans and the hot meat mixture. Bring to a gentle simmer.

Partially cover and cook over low heat for about 2 hours, stirring occasionally. Remove and discard the spice bag. Season to taste with salt. Mix the masa and water, if desired, in a small bowl with a whisk and then stir into the hot chili for thickening. If the chili is too thin, cook a bit longer, uncovered; if it is too thick, add more tomatoes or some water. The longer it simmers, the better it gets.

Transport warm in the Dutch oven, or cool to room temperature, transfer to a covered container, and refrigerate for up to 4 days.

Preparation Timeline: The chili can be made up to 4 days ahead and the salsa can be made 2 days ahead, if refrigerated

Serving Equipment: Large Dutch oven or 6-quart slow cooker, serving ladle, small bowls and spoons for the garnishes

On site/Reheat: Yes

On site/Refrigeration: Optional

Serving Temperature: Hot

CHILI SPICE BAG

3 pinches crushed red pepper flakes

3 whole cloves

1/2 teaspoon whole cumin seeds

2 sprigs oregano

1 bay leaf

6 tablespoons olive oil

4 pounds lean ground beef

3 cloves garlic, minced

6 large yellow onions, chopped

4 bell peppers (any color or combination), chopped

3 (28-ounce) cans whole tomatoes in juice

2 (6-ounce) cans tomato paste

1 (12-ounce) bottle Mexican beer

1/4 cup chili powder

1 jalapeño or serrano chile, seeds and ribs removed, minced

TRANSPORTATION NOTES: Pack the garnishes in covered containers or in resealable plastic bags. If transporting warm, bring the chili in the Dutch oven with a towel wrapped around the base to prevent tipping, or if transporting cold, bring in the covered container.

ON SITE/PREPARATION: Place the chili in the Dutch oven, cover, and reheat over medium-low heat on the stove top, stirring occasionally, until steaming hot. Serve from the stove or transfer to a slow cooker and place on the table, with the garnishes in serving bowls alongside.

4 (14-ounce) cans Anasazi or pinto beans, rinsed and drained

2 (14-ounce) cans baby white beans, rinsed and drained

2 (14-ounce) cans black beans, rinsed and drained

Salt

3 tablespoons masa harina (optional)

$2/3$ cup water (optional)

GARNISHES

Shredded sharp Cheddar cheese

Shredded Monterey Jack cheese or crumbled fresh goat cheese

Shredded iceberg lettuce

Sliced black olives

Sliced avocado

Tomato wedges

Sliced fresh radishes

Sour cream or crema Mexicana

Chopped fresh cilantro

PORK TENDERLOIN with CASSIS SAUCE

SERVES 12 *Always a delightful sight on the buffet table, tenderloin pork roasts are also exceptionally easy to prepare and transport. This delicious, low-fat roast is served with an elegant sauce made from the sweet and viscous black currant liqueur crème de cassis.*

❖ ❖ ❖

Preheat the oven to 375°F. Combine the jelly and dry mustard in a microwave-proof bowl. Place in the microwave on medium heat for 1 to 1¹/₂ minutes to melt and then whisk until smooth.

Tie 2 of the tenderloins together with kitchen twine to make 1 even-sized roast. Repeat with the remaining 2 tenderloins. Place the 2 tied roasts side by side in a large roasting pan and brush them with the jelly glaze. Roast, uncovered, for about 50 minutes, or until the internal temperature reaches 165°F to 170°F (about 25 minutes per pound). Remove the roasts from the oven, cover with foil, and let rest for 15 minutes. (If you are preparing the roasts in advance, once they have rested, wrap them tightly in foil and refrigerate for up to 1 day.)

The roasts can be sliced and arranged at home or on site. To slice, place the roasts on a cutting board and remove the strings. With a sharp knife, diagonally cut the pork into ¹/₂-inch-thick slices and arrange the slices in overlapping rows on a serving platter. Tightly cover and transport warm or refrigerate up to 8 hours until transporting.

Make the sauce right before transporting. Combine the wine, cassis, tarragon, parsley, and peppercorns in a small saucepan. Place the saucepan over medium-high heat and bring to a boil. Cook for about 5 minutes, until reduced by one-third. Pour through a wire mesh to strain and then return to the saucepan, and whisk in the cream. Transfer to a thermos or covered container to transport.

continued

Preparation Timeline: The tenderloin can be roasted and refrigerated up to 1 day ahead, if it will be served cold; make the sauce right before transporting

Serving Equipment: Platter, serving fork, small bowl and ladle for the sauce

On site/Reheat: Yes

On site/Refrigeration: Optional

Serving Temperature: Hot or cold

¹/₂ cup quince or red currant jelly

¹/₂ teaspoon dry mustard

4 (³/₄-pound) whole pork tenderloins

CRÈME DE CASSIS SAUCE

1¹/₂ cups dry white wine

¹/₃ cup crème de cassis liqueur

2 large sprigs tarragon

2 large sprigs parsley

10 black or white whole peppercorns

¹/₃ cup heavy cream or crème fraîche

TRANSPORTATION NOTES: Carry the sauce in the thermos or covered container. Bring the tightly wrapped platter of sliced tenderloin or transport the unsliced baked roasts wrapped whole. Bring a knife and cutting board, if carving on site.

ON SITE/PREPARATION: Reheat the sauce on the stove or in a microwave, then place in a serving bowl with a ladle. Uncover the platter of tenderloins or slice the roasts and arrange on the serving platter. Ladle the warm sauce over the top and serve the extra sauce on the side.

SAUSAGE and APPLE STUFFING CASSEROLE

SERVES 8 *When toting stuffing to a party, it is best to bake it in a casserole rather than trying to fit it into a bird. This side dish is almost a meal in itself. You can use either dried fruit or walnuts, or any combination of the two, because both complement the apples and sausage.*

◆ ◆ ◆

Preheat the oven to 325°F. Place the bread cubes in a single layer on a baking sheet. To dry the bread, bake for about 12 minutes and then transfer to a bowl. Add the poultry seasoning, sage, thyme, and parsley. Leave the oven on, if baking the stuffing immediately.

Place the sausage in a skillet over medium-high heat, breaking it up into small chunks, and cook until no pink remains, 4 to 6 minutes. Remove from the pan with a slotted spoon and add to the bread. Wipe out the skillet with some paper towels, leaving about 2 tablespoons of the fat in the pan. Add the onion and celery and sauté until limp, 5 to 8 minutes, and then add the apples. Cook for 2 minutes longer, until the apples are slightly softened. Add to the bread.

Mix the eggs with ½ cup of the broth and stir into the bread mixture. Add more broth as needed to coat and make a nice moist stuffing. Stir in the 1 cup raisins, cranberries, and/or walnuts. Season to taste with salt and pepper. Butter the baking dish and then mound with the stuffing. (If baking on site, cover and refrigerate until transporting.)

Bake, uncovered, for 1 to 1¼ hours, until crusty brown on top and moist inside.

TRANSPORTATION NOTES: Tightly cover and place the fully baked casserole in a box with towels supporting the sides to prevent tipping.

ON SITE/PREPARATION: Reheat at 300°F, covered, for 20 minutes, until warmed through.

Preparation Timeline: Assemble the day of serving; bake just before transporting; the bread can be dried the day before

Serving Equipment: 9 by 13-inch or 10 by 14-inch casserole or 3-quart gratin dish, knife, spatula

On site/Reheat: Yes

On site/Refrigeration: No

Serving Temperature: Hot or warm

8 to 10 cups challah, French, or country levain bread, in ½-inch cubes

1½ teaspoons poultry seasoning

1 teaspoon minced fresh sage

1 teaspoon minced fresh thyme

¼ cup minced fresh parsley

½ pound bulk pork sausage or sausages with casings removed

1 small yellow onion, minced

3 ribs celery, minced

2 large tart apples, peeled and chopped

2 large eggs, beaten

1¼ cups turkey, chicken, or vegetable broth

1 cup golden raisins, dried or fresh cranberries, and/or walnuts (in any combination), coarsely chopped

Salt and freshly ground black or white pepper

DAY-AFTER-THANKSGIVING POT PIE

SERVES 8 *My friend Bunny Dimmel created this recipe for a day-after-Thanksgiving main meal. "We took it to a potluck supper on Friday," she wrote on a Thanksgiving weekend. "We all liked it better than the Thanksgiving dinner itself." This has to be one of the best leftover dishes ever invented.*

◆ ◆ ◆

To prepare the crust, place the flour, sugar, and salt in a food processor and pulse to combine. Add the shortening and 1/2 cup of the butter and pulse until the size of peas. Add the remaining 1 cup butter, pulse, and then gradually add water until the dough forms a ball. Divide the dough into 2 balls.

Preheat the oven to 350°F if using Pyrex (or 375°F if using a ceramic baking dish). Lightly flour a work surface and then roll out 1 of the dough balls to fit on the bottom and almost up the sides of the baking dish. Line the baking dish with the dough and prick it with a fork all over. Bake in the center of the oven until it just starts to get golden, about 12 minutes. Remove the crust from the oven and let it cool while you assemble the rest of the components. Leave the oven on, if you will be baking the pot pie immediately.

Evenly spread half of the stuffing over the crust. Then make an even layer with half of the turkey and cover with half of the vegetables. Repeat the layers, ending with the vegetables. Pour the warm gravy over the top. Roll out the second ball of dough to just the size of the baking dish for the top crust, and then place it on top, without crimping the edges. (If you are making ahead, the pot pie can be covered with foil and refrigerated at this point for up to 1 day. Allow the casserole to return to room temperature before baking, about 1 hour.)

continued

Preparation Timeline: Can be made up to 1 day ahead, if refrigerated

Serving Equipment: 3-quart oval or 9 by 13-inch baking dish, serving spoon

On site/Reheat: Yes

On site/Refrigeration: No

Serving Temperature: Hot or warm

COUNTRY CRUST

4 1/2 cups white pastry or all-purpose flour

1/4 cup sugar

1 teaspoon salt

1/2 cup vegetable shortening

1 1/2 cups cold unsalted butter, cut into small chunks

3 to 4 tablespoons cold water

4 cups leftover stuffing

4 cups shredded or cut-up cooked turkey (any combination of light and dark meat)

4 cups raw or thawed frozen mixed vegetables (such as peas, corn, and diced carrots)

4 cups turkey gravy, warmed

Bake, uncovered, for 40 to 45 minutes, until the filling is bubbly and the top crust is brown. (The pot pie can also be partially baked for only 30 minutes and finished on site.) Cover and transport warm or leave at room temperature up to 1 hour before transporting.

TRANSPORTATION NOTES: Tightly cover and place in the car in a position to prevent tipping.

ON SITE/PREPARATION: Serve warm or finish baking the partially baked pot pie on site at 350°F for about 20 minutes, until hot and a bit crusty. Serve immediately.

HERBED GREEN BEANS

SERVES 12 *For a meal that needs something green and uncomplicated, try one of my favorite ways of preparing green beans to serve at either a buffet or a holiday dinner. Be sure to choose beans that are firm and blemish free. The size is up to you, but the smaller beans are, the more tender they will be; large beans will take more time to steam to a tender crunch.*

• • •

Bring a large pot of water to a boil over high heat and cook the green beans, covered, until tender-crisp, 5 to 10 minutes (smaller beans will take less time, larger beans, more).

In a skillet over medium-high heat, melt the butter with the oil. Add the onions and celery and sauté until just soft, about 2 minutes. Add the parsley, basil, savory, pepper strips, and salt if desired. Cover and simmer for 5 minutes. Don't let the pepper strips get too soft. Add the green beans to the skillet and toss with tongs. Transfer to the shallow casserole, arrange so the beans face the same direction, and cover tightly. (If making ahead, the beans can be refrigerated at this point for up to 1 day.)

TRANSPORTATION NOTES: Tightly cover and place in a position to prevent tipping.

ON SITE/PREPARATION: Serve at room temperature or reheat in the oven at 350°F for 10 minutes, until warmed through.

Preparation Timeline: Can be made up to 1 day ahead, if refrigerated

Serving Equipment: Shallow casserole dish or serving platter (ovenproof or microwave-proof, depending on how you like to reheat), oversize serving spoon

On site/Reheat: Optional

On site/Refrigeration: No

Serving Temperature: Warm or room temperature

2 pounds fresh green beans, trimmed

1/4 cup butter

1/4 cup olive oil

3 to 4 small white boiling onions, minced

1/2 cup minced celery

1/2 cup minced fresh parsley

1 teaspoon dried basil

1/2 teaspoon dried savory or marjoram

1 red bell pepper, cut into strips

1 teaspoon salt (optional)

SWEET POTATO TORTA with APPLE, PARMESAN, and FRESH THYME

SERVES 8 *Pairing sweet potatoes with something other than marsh-mallows may come as a revelation to some, says food writer Peggy Fallon, who created this dish for this book. The slightly sophisticated treatment with herbs, apples, and Parmesan cheese looks as good as it tastes and is a welcome addition to any holiday gathering. Use a man-doline or the slicing disk on a food processor to make uniform 1/8-inch-thick slices of apples and potatoes for best results.*

◆ ◆ ◆

Melt the butter in a small saucepan or in the microwave. Generously brush a 9-inch cake pan or springform pan with some of the melted butter. If using a springform pan, wrap foil around the outside to pre-vent leaking. Place the thyme sprig in the center of the pan. Preheat the oven to 375°F.

In a bowl, combine the chopped thyme, green onions, Parme-san, flour, salt, sugar, and pepper. Toss to blend well.

Carefully arrange a single layer of sweet potato slices in concen-tric circles, overlapping slightly, without disturbing the thyme garnish in the center of the pan. (This layer will be visible when the torta is unmolded.) Next, evenly layer with half of the apple slices. Sprinkle with about 2 tablespoons of the Parmesan mixture and drizzle with about 2 teaspoons of the butter. Use half of the remaining sweet potatoes to make the next layer, top with the remaining apple slices and the remaining Parmesan mixture, and drizzle with butter. End with a layer of the remaining sweet potatoes and drizzle again with butter. Press down gently to flatten.

continued

Preparation Timeline: Can be prepared up to 1 day ahead, if refrigerated

Serving Equipment: Serving platter, knife, pie server or spatula

On site/Reheat: Optional

On site/Refrigeration: No

Serving Temperature: Warm

3 tablespoons unsalted butter

1 1/2 teaspoons chopped fresh thyme, plus a sprig for garnish

1/2 cup thinly sliced or chopped green onions, white and green parts

1/2 cup freshly grated Parmesan cheese

1 tablespoon flour

3/4 teaspoon salt

1/2 teaspoon sugar

Freshly ground black pepper

1 1/2 pounds red-skinned sweet potatoes (yam variety), peeled and thinly sliced

1 large tart green apple, such as Granny Smith, peeled and thinly sliced

Cover the pan with aluminum foil and bake until the potatoes are just tender, about 45 minutes. Remove the foil and continue baking, uncovered, until lightly browned at the edges, 25 to 30 minutes longer. (If preparing in advance, allow the torta to cool, cover, and leave at room temperature for 1 hour or refrigerate for up to 1 day.)

TRANSPORTATION NOTES: Tightly cover and place in the car in a position to prevent tipping.

ON SITE/PREPARATION: If the torta has been refrigerated, reheat on site, covered, at 375°F until heated through, about 30 minutes. Let the hot torta sit for at least 5 minutes before unmolding. To serve, invert the warm torta onto a serving platter and cut into pie-shaped wedges.

SCALLOPED POTATOES with SAGE

SERVES 12 TO 16 *One Easter, my little sister, a fabulous cook, declared she was making low-fat scalloped potatoes. "Ugh!" was the universal response. Well, with her usual aplomb, she made the following recipe. These potatoes were the star of the buffet. Don't use russet baking potatoes, which won't hold their shape.*

◆ ◆ ◆

Preheat the oven to 450°F. Spray or brush a large baking sheet with oil. Arrange the onion slices and garlic cloves on the pan. Spray or brush the vegetables with olive oil to coat lightly. Roast for about 15 minutes, until a bit browned on the edges and slightly tender. Turn the onion slices halfway through cooking and make sure that the garlic does not burn (if it is past pale golden, remove it and set aside). Remove the vegetables from the oven and let them cool on the pan to room temperature. Coarsely chop the roasted garlic and place it in a small bowl. Decrease the oven temperature to 425°F.

Place the milk in a saucepan over medium-high heat and warm until small bubbles appear around the edge of the pan. Rub the baking dishes with butter. Divide half of the potatoes between the casseroles, placing them in an overlapping layer. Divide half of the onion slices between the dishes and layer them over the potatoes. Sprinkle with the chopped garlic and the sage and season lightly with salt and pepper. Repeat the layers with the remaining vegetables. Slowly add the milk to each casserole to cover three-quarters of the layers (if you overfill, the casseroles will be soupy). Dot the tops with the butter.

Bake for 1 hour to 1 hour 10 minutes, until dotted with brown spots on top and tender when pierced with the tip of a knife. The milk will bubble up and collect around the sides, so occasionally use a spoon to pour it back into the center. The potatoes can stand at room temperature up to 4 hours. Cover to transport.

TRANSPORTATION NOTES: Tightly cover and prevent tipping.

ON SITE/PREPARATION: Reheat, if desired, covered with foil, at 350°F for 15 minutes, until warm.

Preparation Timeline: Can be assembled and baked up to 4 hours ahead and left at room temperature until serving

Serving Equipment: Two 3-quart oval or 9 by 13-inch baking dishes, serving spoon

On site/Reheat: Optional

On site/Refrigeration: No

Serving Temperature: Hot, warm, or room temperature

4 large yellow onions, sliced ¼ inch thick

10 whole cloves garlic, peeled

Olive oil, for brushing

3 cups fat-free milk

4 pounds large white boiling potatoes, peeled and sliced ¼ inch thick

¼ cup finely minced fresh sage

Salt and a few grinds black or white pepper

3 tablespoons unsalted butter

GREEN ONION and SPINACH FRITTATA

SERVES 8 *This lovely and scrumptious spinach soufflé is food writer Lou Pappas's favorite bring-to-the-buffet dish. There is virtually no prep time and no beaten egg whites to fold in: just stir together and pour into the baking dish. Cover and bake on site if you can, so that the frittata is still puffy. It can be cut into squares and served as a side dish or a light vegetarian main course.*

❖ ❖ ❖

Preheat the oven to 350°F. Brush the baking dish with olive oil.

Heat the 1 tablespoon olive oil in a large skillet over medium heat. Add all the onions and sauté until glazed, 1 to 2 minutes. Add all the spinach and sauté for 1 minute. Remove the pan from the heat and add the parsley and tarragon. Season with salt and pepper. Set aside to cool to room temperature.

In a large bowl, beat the eggs until light yellow and mix in the yogurt, the Jarlsberg, and the cooled onion mixture. Pour into the baking dish and sprinkle with the Parmesan. Bake in the oven for 25 to 30 minutes, until browned on top and set throughout.

TRANSPORTATION NOTES: Tightly cover and place in a position to prevent tipping.

ON SITE/PREPARATION: Serve at room temperature or reheat at 300°F for about 15 minutes, until heated through. Or bake on site according to the directions above.

Preparation Timeline: Can stand for 1 hour at room temperature; best if baked on site

Serving Equipment: 3-quart oval or 9 by 13-inch baking dish, serving spoon

On site/Reheat: Optional

On site/Refrigeration: No

Serving Temperature: Warm or room temperature

1 tablespoon olive oil, plus more for brushing

1 large yellow onion, finely chopped

2 bunches green onions, white parts and 4 inches of the green tops, finely chopped

2 (10-ounce) packages frozen chopped spinach, thawed and squeezed dry

1/3 cup minced fresh flat-leaf parsley

1 tablespoon minced fresh tarragon or oregano

Salt and freshly ground black or white pepper

12 large eggs

1/2 cup plain yogurt

2 cups (6 ounces) shredded Jarlsberg or sharp Cheddar cheese

1/2 cup grated or shredded Parmesan cheese

HEARTY WINTER FARE

BUFFET SALMON en CROÛTE

SERVES 16 (MAKES 2 PASTRIES) *Puff pastry is a culinary secret weapon for making knockout dishes. Once the realm of only the most dedicated cooks, now frozen pastry is not only easily found in just about every supermarket, but is also easy to manipulate—and the flavor is comparable to the rarely made-at-home version.*

◆ ◆ ◆

To prepare the mushrooms, melt the butter over medium-high heat in a large skillet. Add the mushrooms and shallots and sauté until well cooked and all the liquid has evaporated, about 10 minutes. Season to taste with salt and pepper. Transfer to a covered container and refrigerate until completely cold, up to 1 day in advance.

To prepare the spinach and garlic, heat the olive oil over medium heat in a skillet. Add the garlic and sauté until soft but not browned, about 1½ minutes. Add the spinach and stir until hot. Season to taste with salt. Transfer to a covered container and refrigerate until completely cold, up to 1 day in advance.

Lightly flour a clean work surface and set out the chilled puff pastry. Let the pastry sit just long enough to become pliable, so it won't break or crack when you unfold it; puff pastry is easiest to work with chilled because it will stretch and tear at room temperature. Be prepared to chill the pastry anytime it becomes warm by clearing part of a shelf in the refrigerator for the baking sheet.

Line 1 or 2 large baking sheets with parchment paper (important because it will absorb the excess butter from the pastry while baking). With a sharp knife, carefully cut the salmon fillet in half lengthwise into 2 equal portions. Drain off any accumulated liquid from the mushroom and the spinach mixtures and then set them to the side of your workspace. In a small bowl, combine the egg and water for the egg wash and beat with a fork until foamy.

continued

Preparation Timeline: **Can be prepared up to 1 day ahead, if refrigerated; bake the day of serving**

Serving Equipment: **Long platter, nice cutting board, or 15-inch rectangular slab of marble; sharp knife, serving spatula**

On site/Reheat: **Optional**

On site/Refrigeration: **No**

Serving Temperature: **Warm or room temperature**

MUSHROOM DUXELLES

¼ cup unsalted butter

1½ pounds fresh mushrooms, coarsely chopped

3 large shallots, chopped

Salt and freshly ground black or white pepper

SPINACH AND GARLIC

1 tablespoon olive oil

2 cloves garlic, minced

2 (10-ounce) packages frozen spinach, thawed and squeezed dry

Salt

Unfold 1 of the sheets of the chilled puff pastry with the longer edge facing you; do not roll out. Mentally make a note of the middle of the pastry; you will be working with the bottom half (the top half will be folded over the salmon). Working quickly and being attentive to the temperature of the pastry, spread half of the spinach mixture over the bottom half of the pastry, leaving a 1-inch border on all sides. Spread half of the mushroom mixture over the top of the spinach and then lay 1 of the salmon fillets on top. Season with salt and pepper and sprinkle with some of the dill.

With a pastry brush or your fingers, moisten the edges of the pastry all the way around with the egg wash, being careful not to let the egg drip down the side (the egg wash will glue the layers together and interfere with the rising). Fold the top half of the pastry over the salmon, so that the top edges line up perfectly with the bottom edges. Press the edges firmly together on all three sides and then crimp with the tines of a fork. (To avoid warming the pastry, don't handle the dough with your fingers more than is necessary.) Transfer the pastry with a metal spatula to the lined baking sheet. Repeat with the remaining ingredients. Place both pastries on 1 baking sheet if they can fit without touching each other; otherwise place on separate baking sheets.

With the tip of a knife, create a steam hole in the top of each pastry and in a few places along the edge. For a shiny, golden surface, brush the tops with the egg wash, being careful not to let the egg drip down the edges of the pastry, and cover loosely with plastic wrap. Place in the refrigerator and chill for at least 1 hour and up to overnight before baking.

1 (1- or 1^1/$_4$-pound) package puff pastry, thawed in the refrigerator overnight

1 (2- to 2^1/$_2$-pound) tail-end salmon fillet, skinned

1 large egg

2 teaspoons water

Salt and freshly ground black or white pepper

1 bunch fresh dill, chopped (optional)

To bake, preheat the oven to 450°F. (The oven needs to be very hot before you put the pastry in, to ensure it rises properly.) Remove the plastic wrap, place the baking sheet on the center rack of the oven, and bake for 15 minutes. Decrease the temperature to 350°F and bake an additional 15 to 20 minutes, until the pastry is golden brown and puffed. Remove from the oven and let rest for at least 30 minutes before cutting. Cover with foil to transport.

TRANSPORTATION NOTES: Tightly cover on a baking sheet and place in a position to prevent tipping or sliding.

ON SITE/PREPARATION: Excellent served at room temperature. Or reheat, uncovered, at 300°F for 10 minutes. Transfer from the baking sheet to the serving platter. Cut into servings or let guests slice their own.

MOROCCAN CHICKEN with DRIED FRUIT and OLIVES

SERVES 16 *Moroccan tagines, or meat and vegetable stews, are festive and colorful main dishes that never fail to pique the palate. Some tagines are quite complex and time consuming to assemble, but this is one of the fastest chicken dishes ever, and it combines all the traditional sweet-tart casbah flavors of capers, dried fruit, olives, sugar, wine, and vinegar. I serve this dish with a big bowl of plain couscous for soaking up the juices.*

• • •

Prepare the chicken the day before baking. In a very large plastic container with a snap-on lid, combine the wine, brown sugar, vinegar, oil, marjoram, and garlic. Add the chicken, olives, apricots, prunes, and capers; cover and shake to coat the chicken with the marinade. Refrigerate overnight.

To serve at room temperature, bake the day of serving. To serve cold, bake the day before and refrigerate overnight. I usually bake this juicy dish on site, since it is easiest to transport in the marinade container and it is delicious served piping hot.

Preheat the oven to 400°F, if baking immediately. Divide the chicken and marinade between the 2 baking dishes. Bake, uncovered, for 35 to 45 minutes, depending on the thickness of the meat, until the chicken is no longer pink when pierced at its thickest part with the tip of a knife. (If using 1 small oven, carefully switch the position of the pans halfway through cooking, or bake 1 pan at a time.) Taste the juices for seasoning. If serving cold, cool to room temperature in the juices, cover, and refrigerate overnight.

continued

Preparation Timeline: **Prepare the entire dish in its marinade and refrigerate overnight before baking; can be baked up to 1 day ahead, if refrigerated**

Serving Equipment: **Two 10 by 15 by 2-inch casseroles, serving fork, oversize spoon or ladle**

On site/Reheat: **Optional**

On site/Refrigeration: **Optional, only if you are not baking the raw chicken immediately (I always place the dish in the oven immediately when I arrive since after baking it can stand at room temperature in the sugar and vinegar)**

Serving Temperature: **Hot or room temperature**

1 cup dry white wine

1 cup (packed) light brown sugar

1/2 cup red or white vinegar (such as merlot or Champagne vinegar)

1/2 cup olive oil

3 tablespoons crumbled dried marjoram or basil

6 cloves garlic, pressed

4 1/2 to 5 pounds boneless, skinless chicken thighs or breasts, rinsed and patted dry

1 (6-ounce) can black, niçoise, or kalamata olives, drained and pitted

1 (6-ounce) can pitted green olives

8 dried apricot halves

8 ounces pitted prunes (regular or bite-size)

1/2 cup drained nonpareil capers

TRANSPORTATION NOTES: If carrying to the potluck already baked, be sure to cover tightly since there is a lot of liquid. Wrap the casserole dish in a large, thick towel and place it on the floor of the car or in the trunk to prevent it from tipping over and the liquid sloshing out. If baking on site, bring the baking dishes and carry the chicken in the plastic container in a position to prevent tipping.

ON SITE/PREPARATION: Reheat, if desired, uncovered at 300°F for 20 minutes, until just warmed through. If baking on site, follow the baking instructions above. Serve hot, or let stand, covered, on the counter for up to 4 hours to serve at room temperature. Serve with a little ladle for the juices.

GREEN BEANS AMANDINE

SERVES 12 *Green Beans Amandine is a beloved holiday vegetable dish. Tossed with slivered almonds, it contains all the mineral salts, vitamins, proteins, fats, and carbs you need for health. All this in a few big bites! Be sure to toast the almonds: this step is crucial to the lovely full flavor of this simple side dish.*

◆ ◆ ◆

Bring a pot of water to a rolling boil and plunge the green beans into it for 15 seconds to set the color. Drain, reserving ³/₄ cup of the water.

In a large skillet, melt 6 tablespoons of the butter over medium heat. Add the reserved hot water, lemon juice, salt, and cayenne. Add the green beans and cook until the liquid has evaporated, 15 to 20 minutes. In another skillet, melt the remaining 6 tablespoons butter over medium-high heat and add the almonds. Cook until the nuts are golden, about 5 minutes. Transfer the green beans to the shallow casserole. Pour the toasted almonds and butter over the top and toss to coat.

TRANSPORTATION NOTES: Tightly cover and place in a position to prevent tipping.

ON SITE/PREPARATION: Reheat to serve hot. The almonds can be prepared on site and tossed with the green beans right before serving.

Preparation Timeline: Can be made up to 1 day ahead, if refrigerated

Serving Equipment: Shallow casserole dish or serving platter (ovenproof or microwave-proof, depending on how you like to reheat), oversize serving spoon

On site/Reheat: Yes

On site/Refrigeration: No

Serving Temperature: Hot or warm

3 pounds fresh green beans, trimmed and thinly sliced on the diagonal

12 tablespoons (³/₄ cup) butter

Juice of ¹/₂ lemon

2 teaspoons salt

Few pinches of cayenne or ground white pepper

2 cups slivered blanched almonds

SPINACH CANNELLONI

SERVES 8 (2 CANNELLONI PER PERSON) *Easily confused with manicotti, another tube-shaped stuffed-pasta dish, cannelloni are made with tender crêpes instead of pasta. While this version is made with chicken, you can substitute cooked turkey, ham, crabmeat, or ground veal. You can also leave out the meat or crab altogether for a vegetarian feast.*

◆ ◆ ◆

To make the tomato sauce, heat the oil in a large skillet over medium-high heat. Add the onion and sauté until soft, 3 to 4 minutes. Add the tomatoes, basil, and sugar and season to taste with salt and pepper. Bring to a simmer and then decrease the heat to low and cook, uncovered, for about 20 minutes, until thickened. Purée the sauce with an immersion blender or in a food mill or food processor. Season to taste with salt. (If making ahead, cool and refrigerate for up to 2 days, or freeze for up to 1 month.)

To make the crêpe batter, place the eggs, milk, water, oil, flour, and salt in a bowl, a blender, or the bowl of a food processor. Whisk, blend, or beat on high until smooth, about 30 seconds. Scrape down the sides and bottom of the bowl once. Blend 15 seconds longer; the batter should have the consistency of heavy cream. Cover and refrigerate for 1 hour or up to overnight. Bring the batter back to room temperature and stir before continuing, adding 1 to 2 tablespoons more water, if needed.

To make the crêpes, spread out a large kitchen towel on the counter. Using a paper towel, brush an 8-inch crêpe pan, skillet, or nonstick frying pan with butter or oil and heat over medium-high heat until hot, but not smoking. Remove the pan from the heat and immediately ladle 3 tablespoons of the batter into 1 side of the pan. Tilt and rotate the pan quickly in all directions to coat the entire surface evenly with the batter. Return the pan to the heat and cook for 1 to 1½ minutes, until the edges are lightly browned and lift up

Preparation Timeline: Sauce and crêpes can be made up to 2 days before assembling, if refrigerated, or 1 month ahead, if frozen; the cannelloni can be assembled up to 2 days ahead, if refrigerated; bake the day of serving

Serving Equipment: 4-quart baking pan, 15 by 10 by 2-inch shallow casserole dish, or two 9 by 13-inch baking dishes; serving spatula

On site/Reheat: Yes

On site/Refrigeration: No

Serving Temperature: Hot or warm

TOMATO SAUCE

2 tablespoons olive oil

1 yellow onion or 3 shallots, finely chopped

1 (28-ounce) can Italian-style plum tomatoes, drained

½ teaspoon crumbled dried basil or marjoram

Pinch of sugar

Salt and freshly ground black or white pepper

CRÊPE BATTER

2 large eggs

⅔ cup milk

⅔ cup (or more) water

1 tablespoon olive oil

1 cup all-purpose flour

¼ teaspoon salt

Melted unsalted butter or vegetable oil, for brushing the pan slightly off the pan and the top is set and almost dry. Slide a long spatula under and turn carefully to prevent tearing. Cook the second side briefly, just until brown in spots but not until crispy, no more than 30 seconds. The crêpes should remain soft, so don't overcook. Invert the pan over the towel to release the crêpe. Continue to make the crêpes in this manner, stirring the batter and oiling the pan lightly as needed before cooking each pancake.

If using within a few hours, simply cover the crêpes with another towel. If you are not going to use the crêpes right away, stack them layered between sheets of parchment paper, place in a resealable plastic bag, and refrigerate for up to 2 days, or freeze in a plastic freezer bag for up to 1 month. (Let the refrigerated crêpes stand at room temperature for 1 hour before filling, so they won't tear when you separate them. If frozen, the crêpes must be thawed in the refrigerator or on the kitchen counter and brought to room temperature before separating to avoid tearing.)

To make the spinach filling, trim any fat and gristle off the chicken, then rinse with cold water. Place in a small saucepan. Add enough water to cover by $1/2$ inch (the exact amount will depend on the size of the pan). Place over medium heat and bring to a simmer. Decrease the heat to low and cook, partially covered, until the chicken is white throughout but still juicy, about 12 minutes. Remove from the heat and let stand in the liquid, uncovered, for 15 minutes. If using immediately, transfer to a plate until cool enough to handle. (Or let cool completely in the liquid, then refrigerate in the liquid for up to 2 days.)

Place the green onions, garlic, and parsley in a food processor and pulse to mince. Add the chicken in pieces and pulse to chop. Transfer to a bowl. Add the eggs and spinach to the processor (no need to wash it out) and combine with a few pulses. Process for 45 to 60 seconds to purée. Add the ricotta, salt, and nutmeg and process for 20 seconds. Add to the meat mixture in the bowl and stir to combine. (If not filling the crêpes right away, cover and refrigerate up to 2 days.)

continued

SPINACH FILLING

1 (6-ounce) boneless skinless chicken breast

About $1/2$ cup water or chicken broth, or a combination

3 green onions, cut into thirds, white and green parts

1 small clove garlic, peeled

$1/2$ cup fresh flat-leaf parsley leaves

2 large eggs

2 (10-ounce) packages frozen spinach, thawed and squeezed dry

$1^1/2$ cups ricotta cheese

$1/4$ teaspoon salt

$1/4$ teaspoon ground nutmeg

MOZZARELLA MORNAY SAUCE

6 tablespoons unsalted butter

$1/3$ cup all-purpose flour

3 cups milk

Pinch of freshly ground white pepper

2 ounces shredded or finely diced mozzarella cheese (about $1/2$ cup)

$1/2$ cup shredded or grated Parmesan cheese

To make the Mornay sauce, melt the butter in a heavy saucepan over medium heat. Add the flour and stir with a whisk until smooth. Cook for 30 seconds, stirring constantly, until bubbly. Add the milk and white pepper. Cook over medium heat, stirring constantly, until the mixture comes to a boil and thickens. Decrease the heat to low and simmer for 1 minute. Add the mozzarella and Parmesan cheeses. Stir to melt. Remove from the heat and cover with waxed or parchment paper to prevent a skin from forming. Refrigerate if not using right away.

To assemble the cannelloni, preheat the oven to 375°F, if baking immediately. Pour the tomato sauce into the baking dish. Lay the crêpes out on a work surface with the more attractive side down. Divide the spinach filling equally between 16 crêpes and roll them up. Place them seam-side down in a single layer in the casserole. Cover with the Mornay sauce. (If making ahead, the cannelloni can be covered with foil at this point and refrigerated for up to 2 days.)

Bake, uncovered, for 40 to 45 minutes, until bubbling-hot and browned on top. Serve or transport hot from the oven or warm, or cool to room temperature, cover, and refrigerate.

TRANSPORTATION NOTES: Tightly cover and place the casserole on the floor of the car or in the trunk with a large thick towel wrapped around the base to prevent tipping, or place in an insulated cooler for longer transport.

ON SITE/PREPARATION: Reheat, covered, at 325°F, for about 20 minutes, until heated through. Remove the cover and bake 5 minutes longer. Serve hot or warm.

MAPLE CANDIED YAMS

SERVES 12 *One of my favorite restaurants is Parcel 104, in the Marriot hotel in Santa Clara, California. It is the creation of chef and entrepreneur Bradley Ogden. I met Brad when he had just started his first restaurant in Marin County. This super-simple side dish is an adaptation of one of Brad's creations, with more butter and sauce for a heavier glaze. I use Garnet yams, but any dark-fleshed sweet potato will do.*

◆ ◆ ◆

Preheat the oven to 375°F, if baking immediately (if using Pyrex, heat to 350°F). Combine the apple juice, brown sugar, maple syrup, molasses, butter, cinnamon, and allspice in the baking dish. Stir with a whisk to combine and spread the mixture to cover the bottom of the casserole. With a large spoon, scoop out ¼ cup of the sauce and set aside in a bowl. Dip the yam slices into the butter mixture to coat both sides and then arrange them, overlapping, to fill the pan (about 2 layers). Pour the reserved sauce over the top. (If making in advance, the dish can be covered and refrigerated at this point.)

Cover tightly with foil and bake for 45 minutes, until tender when pierced with the tip of a knife. Remove the foil and season with salt and pepper. Bake an additional 20 to 30 minutes, uncovered, until browned and bubbly. Let stand at room temperature.

TRANSPORTATION NOTES: Tightly cover and place in a position to prevent tipping.

ON SITE/PREPARATION: Reheat, covered, at 350°F for 15 to 20 minutes, to warm and melt the syrup.

Preparation Timeline: **Prepare the day of serving**

Serving Equipment: **9 by 13-inch or 10 by 10 by 2-inch baking dish, serving spoon**

On site/Reheat: **Yes**

On site/Refrigeration: **No**

Serving Temperature: **Hot or warm**

³/4 cup apple juice

¹/2 cup (packed) light brown sugar

¹/2 cup maple syrup

4¹/2 tablespoons molasses

¹/2 cup butter, melted

¹/2 teaspoon ground cinnamon

¹/4 teaspoon ground allspice

4¹/2 pounds yams or sweet potatoes, peeled and cut into ¹/2-inch-thick slices

Salt and freshly ground black or white pepper

ZUCCHINI, TURKEY, and WILD RICE CASSEROLE

SERVES 10 *The first time my mother described this dish to me, I was skeptical because it uses condensed canned soup and I am a make-it-from-scratch cook. But one bite and it became a favorite, and I have since served it to many distinguished catering clients (including a newly appointed supreme court justice, decades ago). I tried to make the sauce from scratch, omitting the soup, but it never tasted as good or had the right consistency.*

◆ ◆ ◆

In a bowl, combine the sour cream, soup, chiles, parsley, green onions, and marjoram and beat until smooth with a whisk. Season to taste with salt and pepper.

In a saucepan, combine the wild rice with the water and bring to a boil over high heat. Cover, decrease the heat to low, and simmer for 45 minutes, until tender. Drain, if necessary. Set aside to cool.

Bring 1 inch of water to a boil in another saucepan over medium heat. Add the zucchini and steam until barely cooked but still firm, about 8 minutes.

Brush the baking dish with oil or butter. Preheat the oven to 350°F, if baking immediately. Arrange the rice in the bottom of the casserole dish, and using a rubber spatula, cover the entire layer with half of the sauce. Arrange the turkey in an even layer over the sauce, follow with the zucchini, and then cover with the grated cheese. Sprinkle the tomatoes over the cheese and cover with the remaining sauce. (If making ahead, the casserole can be covered with foil and refrigerated at this point for up to 1 day.)

Bake, covered, for 25 minutes. Remove the cover and bake for 20 minutes more, until bubbling-hot. Transport hot from the oven or cool and cover with foil.

continued

Preparation Timeline: **Can be made up to 1 day ahead, if refrigerated; best if baked on site and served straight from the oven**

Serving Equipment: **3- to 4-quart decorative baking dish or 9 by 13-inch casserole dish, serving spatula**

On site/Reheat: **Yes**

On site/Refrigeration: **Optional**

Serving Temperature: **Hot**

SAUCE

3 1/2 cups sour cream

2 (10 3/4-ounce) cans condensed cream of chicken soup

1 (4-ounce) can diced green chiles

1/2 cup chopped fresh parsley

1/4 cup chopped green onions, white and some of the green parts

1 1/2 teaspoons dried crumbled marjoram or oregano

Salt and freshly ground black pepper

1 1/2 cups raw wild rice, rinsed well and drained

4 cups water

2 pounds zucchini, sliced, or 2 (9-ounce) packages frozen artichoke halves, thawed

About 4 cups chopped cooked turkey

2 1/2 cups (about 10 ounces) grated Monterey Jack cheese

1 (28-ounce) can peeled tomatoes, drained and chopped

TRANSPORTATION NOTES: Tightly cover and place the casserole on the floor of the car or in the trunk with a large thick towel wrapped around the base to prevent tipping, or place in an insulated cooler for longer transport.

ON SITE/PREPARATION: Reheat, covered, at 350°F for 20 minutes, or until the casserole is heated through and the cheese is melted. Or for best results, bake on site. Allow the chilled uncooked casserole to return to room temperature and then bake according to the instructions above. Serve hot from the oven.

WINTER CORN PUDDING

SERVES 8 *One year my mother asked me to bring a vegetable side dish for Thanksgiving. I brought the ingredients for this corn pudding and whipped the entire recipe up in five minutes with an immersion blender, put it in a baking dish, and an hour later, we had a superb hot corn pudding. This is a winter corn pudding because it uses creamed corn; you could make a summer one with fresh corn.*

• • •

Lightly butter the baking dish. Preheat the oven to 350°F, if baking immediately.

In a bowl, beat together the eggs, flour, and half-and-half with an electric mixer, whisk, or immersion blender. Season with salt and pepper and add the creamed corn, stirring well with a wooden spoon. Pour into the baking dish, or if baking on site, transfer to a covered container to transport. (If making in advance, the dish can be covered and refrigerated at this point for up to 8 hours. Allow the chilled pudding to return to room temperature, about 30 minutes, before baking.)

Cover with foil and bake for 1 hour, until the pudding is lightly browned and puffed but still quivers in the center.

TRANSPORTATION NOTES: If transporting hot, tightly cover and place in a box with towels packed around the dish to prevent tipping.

ON SITE/PREPARATION: Serve warm, reheating at 350°F for 10 minutes, if necessary.

Preparation Timeline: **Prepare and bake the day of serving**

Serving Equipment: **1¹/₂-quart shallow casserole or 8 by 8-inch baking dish, spatula**

On site/Reheat: **Optional**

On site/Refrigeration: **No**

Serving Temperature: **Hot or warm**

5 large eggs

2 tablespoons all-purpose flour

¹/₂ cup half-and-half or creamy soy milk

Salt and freshly ground black or white pepper

2 (1-pound) cans creamed corn

GROUND BEEF and NOODLE CASSEROLE

SERVES 12 *Consider this an unfussy version of Italian lasagna with fresh cottage cheese and a nice Wisconsin Cheddar. This recipe calls for dried egg noodles rather than fresh because the dried noodles keep their shape better under the tomatoey meat sauce and cheeses. Simple and old-fashioned, yes. Will there be leftovers? Probably not.*

◆ ◆ ◆

To make the meat sauce, heat the oil in a large skillet over medium-high heat. Add the onion and garlic and sauté until soft, about 5 minutes. Add the ground beef, breaking up clumps as it cooks, until no pink remains, 5 to 7 minutes. Stir in the tomato sauce and wine and season to taste with salt and pepper. Bring to a boil and cook for 10 minutes. Remove from the heat. If making ahead, cool and refrigerate for up to 1 day.

Bring water to a boil in a large saucepan and add a few teaspoons of salt. Add the noodles and cook until al dente, 6 to 8 minutes. In a large bowl, beat the cream cheese with a fork until smooth and fluffy. Add the cottage cheese, sour cream, and green onions and mix until smooth. Drain the noodles and add them to the cream cheese mixture. Use a large rubber spatula to combine. Season to taste with salt and pepper.

Preheat the oven to 350°F, if baking immediately. Spread one-third of the meat sauce in the bottom of the casserole, top with half of the noodles, and continue layering, finishing with the meat sauce. Sprinkle with the Cheddar cheese. (If making ahead, the casserole can be covered with foil at this point and refrigerated for up to 1 day. Allow the chilled casserole to return to room temperature, about 1 hour, before baking.)

Preparation Timeline: The sauce can be prepared up to 1 day ahead and the casserole can be assembled up to 12 hours ahead, if refrigerated

Serving Equipment: 4-quart baking dish or 10 by 10 by 4-inch casserole dish, serving spatula

On site/Reheat: Optional

On site/Refrigeration: No

Serving Temperature: Hot or warm

MEAT SAUCE

1/4 cup olive oil

1 large yellow onion, chopped

2 cloves garlic, minced or pressed

3 pounds lean ground beef

2 (15-ounce) cans tomato sauce

3 tablespoons dry red wine

Salt and a few grinds of black or white pepper

2 pounds medium egg noodles

1 (8-ounce) package cream cheese or Neufchâtel cheese, at room temperature

3 cups small-curd low-fat cottage cheese

1 cup sour cream

1 bunch green onions, chopped, white and green parts

Salt and freshly ground black pepper

2 cups (about 1/2 pound) shredded medium or sharp Wisconsin Cheddar or Colby cheese

Bake, uncovered, for 45 to 55 minutes, until bubbling-hot. Transport hot from the oven or warm. Or cool to room temperature, cover, and refrigerate.

TRANSPORTATION NOTES: Tightly cover and place the casserole on the floor of the car or in the trunk with a large thick towel wrapped around the base to prevent tipping, or place in an insulated cooler for longer transport.

ON SITE/PREPARATION: Reheat, if needed, at 350°F for 10 to 15 minutes, until the casserole is heated through and the cheese has melted. Or bake on site according to the instructions above.

ROASTED WINTER ROOTS with LEMON-CILANTRO CRUMBS

SERVES 12 *Serving people on all sorts of diets, from low-carb to no-fat, and at a loss what to make? Well, roasted vegetables with a bit of balsamic vinegar are here to the rescue. You can vary what vegetables you use, but be sure to have at least ¹/₂ pound per person. These vegetables are so popular that you might want to double or triple the recipe, especially if you want some to reheat for your lunch the next day.*

◆ ◆ ◆

To make the crumbs, cut the zest off the lemon in strips and place them in a food processor with the parsley and cilantro. Pulse to finely chop. Add the bread and process to make coarse crumbs. With a fork, stir in the oil and season with salt and pepper. (If making ahead, this mixture can be stored in a plastic bag in the refrigerator overnight.)

Preheat the oven to 350°F. Spread the crumbs on a baking sheet and bake for about 8 minutes, until crisp and browned. Stir once to brown evenly. Cool and store in a plastic bag at room temperature. Keep the oven set to 350°F, if baking immediately.

Place all the vegetables in a single layer in a large baking dish or roasting pan (you may need more than 1 dish). Sprinkle with the olive oil. Combine the vinegar, oregano, sugar, and salt and pepper to taste in a bowl and then toss with the vegetables. Cover the pan tightly with foil, pressing down on the vegetables. Cover with a tight lid or another layer of foil.

Preparation Timeline: The crumbs can be prepared up to 1 day in advance, if refrigerated; prepare everything else the day of serving

Serving Equipment: Shallow casserole dish or serving platter (ovenproof or microwave-proof, depending on how you like to reheat), oversize serving spoon

On site/Reheat: Optional

On site/Refrigeration: No

Serving Temperature: Hot, warm, or room temperature

LEMON-CILANTRO CRUMBS

1 large lemon

¹/₂ cup fresh parsley leaves

¹/₂ cup fresh cilantro leaves

5 slices fresh white, whole wheat, or French bread

1 tablespoon olive oil

Pinch of salt

Freshly ground black or white pepper

4 large sweet potatoes, peeled and cut into 1-inch cubes

12 small white or purple potatoes, cut into 1-inch cubes

8 large carrots, diagonally sliced ¹/₄ inch thick

3 large parsnips, diagonally sliced ¹/₄ inch thick

3 rutabagas or turnips, peeled and cut into 1-inch cubes

3 large beets, peeled and cut into 1-inch cubes

Place the pan in the oven and bake for 40 minutes. Carefully remove the lid and foil and increase the temperature to 400°F. Bake an additional 25 to 35 minutes, until the vegetables are tender, crisp, and golden. Toss once with a metal spatula during this last roasting time to prevent sticking. Transport warm or let sit at room temperature for up to 6 hours before transporting.

TRANSPORTATION NOTES: Tightly cover and place in a position to prevent tipping. Bring the lemon-cilantro crumbs in a separate bag.

ON SITE/PREPARATION: Reheat, uncovered, if desired, at 350°F for 15 to 20 minutes. Sprinkle with the lemon-cilantro crumbs right before serving.

2 large red or yellow onions, cut into eighths

6 shallots, peeled and halved or quartered

6 tablespoons olive oil

5 tablespoons balsamic vinegar

2 tablespoons minced fresh oregano, basil, thyme, rosemary, or sage

1 teaspoon sugar

Pinch of salt

Freshly ground black or white pepper

GORGONZOLA BREAD PUDDING

SERVES 8 *Gorgonzola is the name of a town outside of Milan, in northern Italy, where this bluish-green–veined cow's milk cheese was first made. It is now one of the classic flavors of Italian cuisine. Try to find a cheese aged less than six months, so it will not be overpowering. I serve this savory bread pudding with a warm, fresh tomato sauce over the top, but it is good without this extra step, as well.*

◆ ◆ ◆

To make the tomato sauce, heat the oil in a small saucepan over medium-high heat. Add the shallot and cook for 1 or 2 minutes, until softened. Add the tomatoes and wine and bring to a boil. Decrease the heat to low and simmer for 15 minutes, or until thickened. Add the basil and season to taste with salt and pepper. Remove from the heat and cover to keep warm until serving. (If making ahead, the sauce can be cooled to room temperature, transferred to a covered container, and refrigerated for up to 3 days.)

Generously butter a 10-inch springform pan. Wrap some foil around the outside of the pan to prevent leaks. Place a round of parchment in the bottom so that the pudding will release from the pan easily.

Place the bread cubes in a bowl and toss with the basil. Place the half-and-half in a saucepan over medium-high heat and warm until small bubbles appear around the edge of the pan. Add the cheese, garlic, and oil to the pan, stirring until the cheese melts. Remove the pan from the heat and season the mixture with salt and pepper.

Lightly beat the eggs in another bowl and add a few tablespoons of the hot cheese mixture, whisking constantly, to temper the eggs. Slowly pour the egg mixture into the cheese mixture, whisking well. Pour over the bread cubes and toss to coat. Let stand for 15 minutes to allow the bread to absorb the liquid.

Preparation Timeline: The sauce can be prepared up to 3 days ahead, if refrigerated; make the bread pudding the day of serving

Serving Equipment: Large serving plate, knife, serving spatula, small bowl and ladle or pitcher for sauce (optional)

On site/Reheat: Optional

On site/Refrigeration: No

Serving Temperature: Warm or room temperature

TOMATO-BASIL SAUCE (OPTIONAL)

1 tablespoon olive oil

1 shallot, minced

1 (28-ounce) can diced Italian plum tomatoes

2 tablespoons dry red or white wine

2 to 3 tablespoons chopped fresh basil

Pinch of salt and freshly ground black pepper

BREAD PUDDING

1 (1-pound) loaf day-old French bread, cut into 1-inch cubes

2 tablespoons chopped fresh basil

3 cups half-and-half

6 ounces Gorgonzola cheese, crumbled (about 1 1/2 cups)

2 cloves garlic, minced

2 tablespoons extra-virgin olive oil

Salt and freshly ground black pepper

9 large eggs

Preheat the oven to 400°F, if baking immediately. Transfer the soaked bread cubes to the prepared pan. (If preparing ahead, the pudding can be covered and refrigerated at this point for up to 8 hours.)

Bake, uncovered, for about 1 hour, until the pudding is browned, puffed, and set in the center. The baked bread pudding can stand at room temperature for up to 2 hours before transporting.

TRANSPORTATION NOTES: Transport the pudding in the springform pan fully cooked. Bring the sauce in a tightly covered container or microwave-proof bowl.

ON SITE/PREPARATION: Reheat, if desired, at 350°F for 10 to 15 minutes, until heated through. Heat the sauce on the stove or in the microwave. To serve, remove the springform sides and slide the pudding onto a serving plate. Cut into wedges and top with the warm tomato sauce.

INDEX